Basketry:
The Nantucket
Tradition

Published in 1990 by Lark Books
50 College Street
Asheville, North Carolina, U.S.A., 28801

© 1990 by John McGuire

Design and production: Judy Clark
Typesetting: Elaine Thompson

ISBN 0-937274-50-X

Library of Congress Cataloging-in-Publication Data
    Basketry: the Nantucket tradition / by John McGuire;
photography by Henry Peach.
        p.   cm.
Includes bibliographical references and index.
ISBN 0-937274-50-X: $24.95
1. Basket making—Massachusetts—Nantucket Island.
2. Nantucket Island (Mass.)—Industries.   I. Title.
TT879.B3M388   1990
746.41'2'0974497--dc20
                                  89-83931
                                  CIP

10 9 8 7 6 5 4 3 2

Every effort has been made to ensure that all information in this
book is accurate. However, due to differing conditions, tools, and
individual skills, the publisher cannot be responsible for any
injuries, losses, or other damages which may result from the use
of the information in this book.

Basketry: The Nantucket Tradition

History • Techniques • Projects

John McGuire

Photography by Henry Peach

Lark
Books

Dedication

To my family, extended family and friends . . . especially Ellin Ente for her support and encouragement.

Acknowledgements

My appreciation and thanks are extended to all these people who made this book a labor of joy and exploration: Charles and Barbara Adams, Helen Chase, Charles Derby, Dale Duchesne, Ellin Ente, Toni and Charles Frame, Chester Freeman, Lauretta Gibbs, Christine Gregg, PhD., Victoria Taylor Hawkins, curator of the Nantucket Historical Association, Olive Hubbard, Joan Huntington, Wendell Jackson, Henry Peach, Bill and Susan Pope, Douglas Porchette, Steve Robertson, Mary Jo Rushlow, Diane Stanton, Cara Sutherland, and George Wesolowski. I would also like to thank the following groups and organizations: the Islanders of Nantucket Island, the Nantucket Historical Association and Archives, the Nantucket Lightship Preservation, Inc., the New Bedford Whaling Museum and Archives, the Pacific National Bank of Nantucket Island, and the United States Coast Guard Archives.

Contents

Preface

When I first conceived of this book, I thought the Nantucket basket itself would be the complete focus. However, I found it impossible to separate the basket from its historical context. Like all other baskets, the Nantucket originated from necessity, originality and frugality. The interaction of people in commerce and everyday life required baskets as necessities for measures, transport and trade. The originality came from the makers who translated one approach into another. The spark of creativity came from a unique basketmaking approach shaped by social and cultural conditions and limited materials.

Nantucket's survival into the 20th century has been a testament to ingenuity and adaptability. The islanders' legacy to the world has been a fantastic array of artifacts, architecture, history and inspiration. Without belaboring the history of Nantucket, I have attempted to put in perspective some of what the residents enjoyed and endured. In no way does this book attempt to tell it all; others have done far more. It does attempt to place Nantucket baskets into a historical context and to provide another theory for their making.

Unlike many other basket persuasions, Nantucket baskets seem born out of limitations rather than bounty. Off-island basketmakers needed only to move to the next county to find materials or a market. The geography of Nantucket precluded this alternative, at least directly. Materials and approach found in exploration and trade parented the Nantucket basket into existence.

I am sure that some will ask, "Why such a focus on the whaling industry?" The answer is quite simple: whaling was to Nantucket what the lightship was to the basket.

To avoid discussing the whaling industry is to deny the island's heritage. The opening of the Pacific to whaling and trading provided the cane that is utilized in this type of basketry. Also, the nautical aspects of this basket are undeniable. While sailors on whaling ships did not specifically mention basketmaking, the making of rattan baskets in places other than the lightship is fairly well documented. Minimal requirements for tools and space made this trade/craft easily transported and employed.

Moreover, Nantucket's whaling industry required lightships to minimize navigational peril. The duty on board these ships nurtured the manufacture of this rattan basket in greater numbers. Baskets were made in nesting sizes for economy of space and in sufficient numbers to supply an eager market. These products gave rise to the name "lightship baskets," and a continuing marketing genius perpetuates their manufacture.

It is clear to me that a mystique is woven into these special lightship baskets and Nantucket baskets. The details of their making are rather closely guarded. The basketmaking techniques in this book were gleaned from many sources as well as through my own research and experience. And while I do not wish to imply that this is the only way to make such products, it seems to work for me and has worked for the hundreds of students I have taught over the years. It is never my intention to weaken the market for those who make their living in the manufacture of these baskets. In fact, revelation usually produces a more informed client. Regardless of how you use this book, I hope it gives you a special feeling for this unique island and the people who made it great.

Illustration from a whaler's journal. Photo courtesy of the Nantucket Historical Association.

Introduction

It is difficult for the average person to visit Cape Cod and the outer islands of Martha's Vineyard and Nantucket and not sense the history that emerged from this area. Deeply rooted in an era of fishing and whaling, this majestic stretch of coastline and its islands speak proudly of their contributions to the evolution of the nation.

The island of Nantucket has experienced more than its share of the ebb and flow of history. In two different eras, Nantucket caused people to take notice. Today the island has a population that swells to approximately 40,000 in the summer, and some would say that this is a third era, the one that tests the islanders the most.

Of all the contributors to Nantucket's history, perhaps the most significant was the whaling industry. Visions of sailors harpooning these majestic creatures of the deep can produce conflicting emotions, at best; for many people, the sadness of the kill is impossible to overlook.

Evolution of the Reyes oval. Collection of the Nantucket Historical Association.

Yet the scales were not always tipped in favor of the hunters. Many ships were lost at sea, and hundreds of men never returned. Moreover, between 1842 and 1846, at the height of whaling, a comparatively modest 20,000 whales were taken. By contrast, between 1960 and 1964, Russia and Japan took 127,000 whales; this reality may be the harder one to handle.

Today the most recognizable product of the island and its maritime history is probably the Nantucket basket. Despite its endless variations, the essential basket is unmistakable: cane weavers, a wooden bottom, a swinging bail handle and short, wooden ribs. On a recent trip to the island, I was amazed by how many new outlets carry what has been described as "the ultimate basket." Prices ranged from $100 to $3200. I did not even look at the diamond and gold miniatures on display.

The evolution of the Nantucket basket is perhaps its most clouded detail. The need for baskets was obvious, and their nesting sizes provided economy of space. The other components probably resulted from common sense and Yankee ingenuity.

Soon after the settlement of the island, the Wampanoag and other tribes began selling baskets to the white settlers, who had precious little time to produce baskets and who considered basketry unskilled labor, a pick-up trade. These baskets reflected the stylistic interplay between Native American and European cultures, but were woven of black ash instead of more familiar hardwoods. This unique and supple material was easily obtainable off-island and could be fashioned into baskets that functioned as the brown paper bags of the period.

In my opinion, however, the ancestry of the Nantucket basket has more to do with New Hampshire than with the island's native populations. From its very beginnings, Nantucket relied on the determination and resourcefulness of its inhabitants to succeed but on trade with the world to survive. Dwarfed by the prevailing winds, the island's native hardwoods, such as its oaks, were twisted in shape and limited in numbers, hardly conducive to the making of baskets—or the building of houses. While oaks were plentiful along the Massachusetts coast, what is now the oldest house on Nantucket was built with lumber from New Hampshire—clear evidence of early commerce with that colony.[1]

New Hampshire baskets frequently had riveted bail handles—the rivets used in maritime trades easily solved the need for a swing handle—and wooden bottoms. Wooden bottoms are easy to explain. Baskets were important, so important that they were a part of a

New Hampshire farm basket with wooden bottom and riveted bail.

person's estate. They were expensive, relative to the times, and they were expected to last, even to the point of rather fanciful repairs. Consider a basket with a broken bottom, two wooden disks that sandwiches the break for a make-do repair, and a few nails, and you have the start of a new kind of construction. Soon two disks gave way to one with a cut groove. Anyone who has ever prepared the long ribs and weavers for a kicked-up-bottom basket, and who has struggled to start one, will understand the joy of a wooden base.

While the use of forms in the shaping of a Nantucket basket was hardly a new twist in basketmaking, early moulds made from a damaged mast could easily explain the tapering sides and graduated sizes, as well as a resourceful recycling of wood. Add to this creative conservation the cane imported from the Pacific in the early 1800s, an abundance of scrap oak pieces left over from the manufacture of barrels and buckets, sailors with a lot of idle time, and you have another Yankee invention that makes it big.

THE ISLAND AND BASKET:

TRADITION

A Historical Perspective

The unique island of Nantucket, an Indian name meaning "land far out to sea," lies some 30 miles off the coast of Massachusetts. It is an unpretentious land mass of sand, pebbles, and stone, about 15 miles long and three miles wide. While the island is serene in appearance today, its glacial origins were apparently spectacular. As the Great Ice Age gouged and contoured the features of the continent, it carried along in its icy mass the genesis of the islands known as Nantucket and Martha's Vineyard. As the ice melted, the deposits of materials containing a unique medley of soils and plant life became islands surrounded by the melted water of their creator.

Nantucket's earliest inhabitants were Native Americans, but its earliest recorded owner was James Forrett, whose possession resulted from the generosity of the King of England. Apparently unimpressed, Forrett sold the island in 1641 for 40 pounds.

The purchaser was Thomas Mayhew, of Watertown, Massachusetts, whose son was a preacher to the Indians on Martha's Vineyard. In 1659 Mayhew sold 90% of the island to a group of nine Massachusetts Englishmen for 30 pounds and two beaver hats, reserving the tenth share for his son.

The first of this group to inhabit the island was Thomas Macy. Along with his family and two other buyers, Edward Starbuck and Isaac Coleman, Macy moved to Nantucket to raise sheep in a climate not so

Engraving of southeastern view of Nantucket. Drawn by J. W. Barber. Engraved by S. E. Brown, Boston.

religiously zealous. The Puritans who governed Massachusetts were not known for their tolerance, particularly when it came to the independent, anti-authoritarian Quakers. While not a Quaker himself, Macy ran afoul of the authorities when he sheltered Quakers from a thunderstorm. Summarily fined for his actions, threatened with hanging if he committed further heresies, Macy chose to move on.[2]

Anxious to govern the island autonomously, Macy and Tristam Coffin, an innkeeper from Salisbury, applied to the English governor in New York, who had jurisdiction and granted them that status. Five other settlers were made selectmen. The occupations of these men included weaver, tailor, cooper and shoemaker; three were seamen, which suggests how important the sea was to the survival of the Bay State. The ten original proprietors chose partners, who in turn attracted 14 more, described as artisans and mechanics. The early cast of characters included names that would reappear throughout the history of the island: Folger, Coffin, Starbuck, Macy and Gardner, to mention but a few.

The settlers' new home possessed a land character that could be described as unique. Nantucket was blessed with milder winters and cooler summers than the mainland enjoyed, abundant water evident in picturesque ponds, a natural harbor, rich soil and 746 native species of plants. There were deer, quail, rabbit and pheasant, but no squirrel, chipmunk, fox, skunk, porcupine or raccoon. It was in this verdant setting, inhabited by 7,000 Indians of the Wampanoag tribe, who spoke an Algonquin dialect, that the new owners began to leave their permanent imprint.

Raising sheep was their primary goal, and the island seemed perfect to that end. There were no predators except the "wild" dogs that belonged to the Indians. The island's natural barriers allowed the sheep free roam. While that was good for the sheep owners, it was bad for the fragile ecosystem. The animals ate and trampled vegetation that would take decades to reappear.

Jethro Coffin House (1686), built in the familiar lean-to style of the period.

With raising sheep the primary agriculture, spinning and weaving wool cloth became the dominant industry. The islanders prospered and the population grew. In 1671 they established a town called Sherburne on the north shore.

But Nantucket was not without its problems. The peaceful island did not remain tranquil for long. Internal squabbling and repeated disregard for neighbors were the orders of the day. John Gardner and Peter Folger, a Renaissance man of many talents, continually opposed the policies of Chief Magistrate Tristam Coffin. The infighting and disunity would continue to plague the island. While the conflicts were ultimately resolved, the intermarriage of Jethro Coffin and Mary Gardner in 1868 heralded further cooperation. This pattern of marriage among early settlers so bound the bloodlines of the inhabitants that any tragedy inevitably affected many of the islanders.

A second problem was the often despicable treatment of the native population. Constantly harrassed, branded for minor offenses, bullied into selling their lands, the Indians decreased in number as the newcomers thrived. Even their animals were endangered. Convinced that the Indian dogs threatened their sheep, the settlers called constantly for killing them off.[3]

As the 1600s drew to a close, the islanders began to look seaward for an additional source of revenue. Specifically, they began to turn to whaling. The potential was obvious; the Indians were known to kill whales from canoes close to shore. In 1672 Nantucket recruited whaling men to resettle on the island and pay the town five shillings per whale, in exchange for unwooded lands, rights to build and resell if they left, grazing privileges and a period of time they could spend away from whaling.[4] In 1690 Ichabod Paddock was hired to move to Nantucket and teach the islanders how to kill whales and obtain the oil.

The King himself took note of the money to be made from the "Royal Fish." Rules regarding unclaimed, beached drift whales were clearly defined. They were divided into shares: part went to the finder, part to the government and a third remained to be given in disputes. If a kill went unreported, a fine of 20 shillings could be levied, assuming the miscreant was caught.

The inducements to enter whaling and fish transport were significant. The vessels employed in such commerce paid no taxes for seven years, and fishermen were exempt from military service during fishing season. Perhaps most important, in 1699 the Wool Act forbade the sale of wool cloth between colonies. Suddenly, the island found

Old Mill (1746) built by Nathan Wilbur. The top rotates with the help of the fifty-foot mast which travels a stone path.

it necessary to shift gears more fully to the pursuit of the whale and its precious by-products.

Because whales were abundant and virtually without fear of man, whaling was at first concentrated in near coastal waters. A complex set of rules developed for "divvying up" the whales and returning the "irons" (a nickname for harpoons). Coastal whaling was soon so active that the south side of the island was divided into four parts. On each of three half-mile stretches of coastline, whalers erected a tall mast to look out to sea, a hut to house five or six men and a "try works" to cook the raw blubber and obtain the oil.

As the whalers became more aggressive hunters, the whales became warier and moved farther from shore. Their numbers dwindled. Then, in 1712, a captain named Christopher Hussey was blown off course into deep water, where he sighted and took the first sperm whale. This species was larger and more valuable than the bowheads and right whales the islanders has been catching. The high-quality spermaceti, which provided the basis for expensive candles and lamp oil, was extremely profitable.

Between 1712 and 1776, Nantucket developed into an independent power in the whaling trade. Indeed, she eclipsed the whaling might of England, her principal trading partner. In this first great era of Nantucket whaling, several factors were especially significant.

First was the emergence of the Quakers as a dominant force on the island. Initially, the inhabitants did not rush to establish any real religious congregations. Having just escaped the Puritan oligarchy, the nonconforming islanders preferred to keep Nantucket spiritually open.

Quaker Meeting House doorway.

In the waning years of the 1600s, however, John Richardson, a Quaker originally from England, visited Nantucket and liked what he saw. With a few other members of the Society of Friends, he relocated from Newport. With the conversion of Mary (Coffin) Starbuck and her children, the Quakers received a welcome boost. A leading citizen, Starbuck lent the Quakers her prestige as well as her house, where meetings were held for four years.

The basic tenets of the Quaker faith were simplicity, high thinking, plain living, non-worldliness, humility, simple clothes of the best quality, and the avoidance of such frivolities as ornamentation and paint (except for preservation)—values that gave believers the strength and courage to survive deprivations and succeed in their endeavors. During the first quarter of the 18th century, Quakerism took firm root in the island; it went on to become the predominant religion. It would begin to decline only after the church split in the 1830s. The decline would not be complete until the deaths of the last survivors of the Nantucket meeting, James Austin and a woman known simply as Huldah. Her burial in 1900 was the last Quaker funeral.[5]

For more than a century, the Quaker faith dominated the island. Profoundly gifted in commerce, shrewd but honorable in their business dealings, the Quakers soon emerged as the guiding force in the whaling industry. It is said that without the solid ideas of the Quaker faith Nantucket whaling would not have survived.

And survive it did. In 1723 the islanders built Straight Wharf; in 1726 they took 86 whales. As whalers ventured farther and farther from shore, their vessels became larger and larger. The small sloops with as few as 13 hands and two boats became things of the past. With voyages now lasting for weeks, tonnage increased. Longer voyages meant that blubber had to be rendered on board, which meant larger crews, more provisions and more complicated equipment. The expense of underwriting a bigger ship demanded more return on investment—more whale oil and more room to store it. The "shooks" of the hold housed barrels of oil sized to fit everywhere. "Greasy luck"—the money to be made from whaling—was on a "lay" (or share) basis, an arrangement that added to the wealth of the investors and Quaker captains, generating significant wealth for those at the top.

As whaling expanded, so did the trades associated with it. The need for barrels was obvious, and the trade of cooper was a common occupation. (Incidentally, the popularity of this trade has given rise to the mistaken speculation that the Nantucket basket developed out of it. While the ability to make barrels was not a hindrance to manufacturing baskets, neither was it a requirement.) Individual businesses sprang up to meet the demands of oil storage, provisioning the crew and marketing the whaling by-products.

Morgan Whaling Ship, the last commissioned wooden whaling vessel.

During this period the island was a hub of activity. The business of whaling and everyday island living caused flurries of harbor excitement. Imagine the arrival of ships, other ships under sail or about to depart, and the familiar sound of barrels being rolled over cobblestone streets on their way to storage after being unloaded. The stench of wet seaweed covering the barrels to keep them tight probably permeated the air. Even the look of the inhabitants changed. Islanders had intermarried and their children had had children. Newcomers added to the island's population.

Material wealth began to show in ever more obvious ways. While constrained by a predominant Quaker ethic, a growing wealthy class erected finer homes with lush

grounds. Along with their cargoes of bone and oil, ship captains brought back finery and flora for their own use, which added visual textures to an island already caught up in change.

The trade was not without its drawbacks. The American style of whaling—an aggressive, energetic blend of the European reliance on large ships and the native Indians' use of small boats—was extraordinarily dangerous. Men were regularly maimed or killed. In 1724 Elisha Coffin and his ship were lost at sea; in 1731, Master Thomas Hathaway and his vessel; in 1742, Daniel Paddack and his ship. The operations of Spanish privateers and the risk of capture by the French, who fought with England until 1763, added to the dangers on the high seas.

Throughout this entire period, Nantucket dealt with convoluted entanglements with England regarding taxation, duties and lines of authority. George III's bounty on "home port" oil stirred resentment but did not diminish the growth of the whaling industry. As England continued to make it more difficult for the islanders, these venturesome people looked to other markets. In some cases, they emigrated elsewhere to ply their trade.

As Nantucket grew, its determination to remain unencumbered by the political strife that gripped Europe became paramount. For one thing, conflict hampered trade. But both religion and tradition reinforced the island's neutrality. The Quakers were ethically opposed to fighting—indeed, they were exempt from military service, and individual members were "read out" of meetings for carrying arms or serving on an armed vessel. Moreover, from its very beginnings, the island had focused its energies on being independent and unimpeded by politics.

However, not everyone prospered. The people who suffered the most were the Indians. Their initial population of 7,000 declined to 358 by 1764, and a plague in that year further reduced their number to 136. These once-proud people who had owned this most precious and aristocratic of islands were reduced to a handful, and their final extinction was inevitable.

ic Whimsy. This jointed figure does acrobatics as the ...s turned. It was made as a pastime by seamen. ...on of Emmory and Gerry Prior.

For most islanders, however, things worked out well. When the English bought Canada, new whaling grounds opened up. In 1772 a spermaceti candle factory opened on the island. In 1775 Captain Uriah Bunker discovered a bounty of sperm whales off the Brazilian banks.[6] Nantucket, with a harbor, an infrastructure and a fleet of 150 ships employing 2,000 men, took full advantage of the discovery. The sea turned red with the blood of whales, and their oil and bone fueled the industry and the economy of the island. The town of Sherburne was renamed Nantucket and moved to its present location, and the growth of that harbor town reflected the ultimate triumph of whaling and its impact on the island.

Then came the American Revolution—for Nantucket a disaster. While the Quakers were pacifists and politically unaligned, many others were Loyalists. Profoundly mistrusted by both sides, geographically in the path of both belligerents, the islanders lost their ships, their livelihood and, in many cases, their lives.

The great fleet was decimated. During the eight years of war, 134 ships were captured or confiscated, with crews lost, jailed or impressed into service. Before the islanders could rebuild, another 15 ships were lost. The islanders tried valiantly to carry on their whaling and West India trade, but for all intents and purposes maritime activity came to a dead halt.

At one point, the British invaded the island, and the usually open harbor froze in 1779, creating further deprivation and hardship. Even simple firewood was at a premium. So mistrustful were the Colonists that provisions destined for the island required the signatures of three off-island justices of the peace in Barnstable. The contrast to the more affluent days must have been overwhelming. At war's end, Nantucket had suffered losses of more than $1,000,000. Of 800 families, 202 were headed by widows, and there were 342 orphans.

Staggering from the loss of its fleet, Nantucket began to rebuild. But the hard times were not over. To encourage home industry, the English placed high tariffs on imported oil. The fact that Britain was Nantucket's only open market for sperm oil created further hardships. Lower oil prices and a consumer shift away from spermacetti candles to cheaper tallow ones forced some hard-pressed captains to relocate to England, France, Nova Scotia and other foreign ports. Nantucket now faced a growing list of competitors who had fared better during the war and who could lure captains to their employ.

Still, Nantucket rebounded. The shrewd, hard-working bankers and businessmen quickly rebuilt a smaller fleet. When the French Revolution erupted in 1789, with its attendant interruption of the marketing of oil in Europe, many captains who had fled to France returned to Nantucket.

But politics again disrupted the island. During the War of 1812, islanders endured hardships reminiscent of the American Revolution. This time, the fleet was reduced from 116 ships to 23. Yet again, Nantucket rebuilt. While the fleet never again equaled its earlier size, there were 72 vessels by 1820. Twenty years later, there were 86. With this smaller but very powerful fleet, Nantucket entered its second great era of whaling, a heyday of prosperity that lasted from about 1820 to 1850.

Crucial to this Golden Age was access to the Pacific. By the turn of the century, ships were rounding the Cape of Good Hope and sailing as far as Asia. Pacific whaling had profound implications for the Orient, for Nantucket and for the industry itself. The opening up of Asia became the backbone of United States Pacific policy. The ships returned, not only with greasy luck, but with Imari, Chinese jade, opium bottles, silks, souvenirs from the South Seas, and that most humble of imports—cane used to seat chairs and to weave rattan baskets. Who could have predicted that those unique baskets would one day become perhaps the most recognized status symbols on the island?

Voyages to the Pacific lasted, not weeks or months, but four, five, even six years. Such journeys required even larger ships to accommodate men and provisions, with enough cargo room to turn a profit on the enormous investment involved. For example, the good ship *Beaver*, commanded by Captain Paul Worth, was a 240-ton vessel that had been part of the Boston Tea Party. With a crew of 17 men, it carried 40 barrels of salted meat, 24 barrels of flour, 1,000 pounds of rice, 30 bushels of peas and beans, 200 pounds of cranberries to forestall scurvy, and other sundries—provisions that would feed the crew for 17 months before it was necessary to reprovision in foreign ports (a very expensive process indeed).

The cost of underwriting such a venture was upwards of $40,000, half for the ship itself (which was frequently owned by a group of investors) and half for the voyage. With whale oil worth 95 cents a gallon, the return on investment might seem meager. On the contrary: one sperm whale yielded almost 2,000 gallons of oil, and great numbers of whales populated the new grounds. According to old records, two ships alone made $2,000,000 during their careers. Under this kind of impetus, Nantucket ships followed their prey to the four corners of the earth.

Although profits were good, they weren't always handsome. The rich investors and captains took their share first, and what remained for the men who had signed on board was frequently a pittance. In the last

After the opening of the Pacific banks, fine Chinese porcelain was brought back as souvenirs and sold on Nantucket. Collection of Mr. and Mrs. Thomas Harvilla.

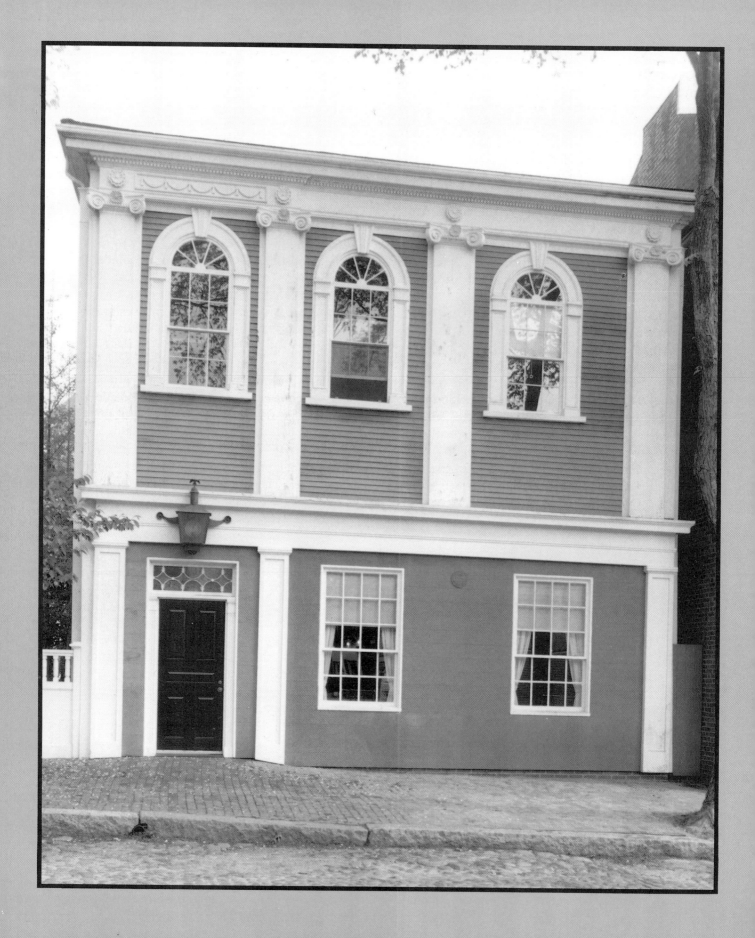

days of whaling, a story circulated about a 16-year-old boy who returned after five years with a share worth 50 cents, and it was probably not exaggerated. Conditions were deplorable. There was a constant risk of fire on board, because of oil-soaked floors and open fires stoked to try out the blubber. There were treacherous reefs, Arctic ice, scurvy, cockroaches, cannibals and rats, not to mention enraged whales that could stave in the side of a ship or pull the men who harpooned them to their deaths (known in the trade as "Nantucket sleigh rides"). The low pay and dangerous working conditions made it difficult to find crews, and many a captain had to settle for a motley mixture of undesirables and potential mutineers.

But for islanders who made their livings around the ships rather than on them, the years between 1820 and 1850 were prosperous ones. Nantucket's wharf was again alive with coopers, sailmakers, carpenters, riggers, ropemakers, canvas weavers, block makers and a myriad of other related businesses. There were now five wharves, and the harbor was dotted with ships at anchor, since only a percentage of the fleet was under sail at any one time. Shops were stocked with the ordinary and the extraordinary. Carriages clattered over the cobblestone streets built from stones used as ships' ballast. Stately homes and buildings with details of great beauty gave the island a distinctive personality.

The ships also returned with holds full of the usual and the unusual. Cargoes included Japanese pines, peonies, poppies, azaleas, ginkgo trees, wisteria, iris and even Napoleonic willows taken from the grave on St. Helena—all of which added further variety to the island.

Nantucket's resurgence was obvious and everywhere. The island's fame was such that in 1835 Daniel Webster described it as a "City at Sea." In these "palmy days" of whaling prosperity, the Quaker ethic crumbled. The simple, finely crafted homes of earlier years gave way to elegant, opulent houses that still stand today. The "Three Bricks," which merchant Joseph Starbuck built for his sons, provided solid evidence of the changes in wealth and its uses.

One well-known example of this break with the more severe architecture is a frame building now owned by the Pacific National Bank. (Incidentally, the name of the bank, founded in 1804 with a capitalization of $100,000, suggests the scope of Nantucket's involvement with the rest of the world.) In 1807 it was described by a visitor as "elegant with Ionic pilasters."[7] The building's upper floors housed Masonic meeting rooms, and its ground floor was commercial. Its present facade shows what is thought to be the work of the American architect Charles Bulfinch and the handwork of those who worked on his famous Boston creations.

As part of the island's prosperity, the Athenaeum Library and Museum opened in 1827, along with two public schools and the private Coffin School. Education was important to the island. Even ships carried small libraries, and captains exchanged books during chance encounters at sea.

As the ethnicity of the island became more varied, sailors from around the world walked Nantucket's streets. The island's black population, slave in origin, provided Nantucket with its first black whaling captain,

The Coffin School, founded in 1827.

Headquarters of the Pacific National Bank.

Absalom Boston. Surprisingly enough, some Quakers "had Negroes" and even willed them to their heirs.[8] In fact, it was the heated issue of slavery that ultimately drove some Quakers to take up arms and fight with the Union in the Civil War.

By the time the opening shot was fired in 1860, Nantucket's whaling industry was virtually dead and the island itself was in decline. Sperm whales were over-hunted, and competition was fierce for the dollars to be made from them. Crews became increasingly difficult to enlist, and those who did sign on board frequently deserted or mutinied to obtain passage to the California gold fields. Market demand for oil began to slip with the development of kerosene in 1836 and the use of coal gas for European lamps. When the first petroleum wells were drilled in Pennsylvania, the government began using cheaper coal oils for the lighthouses and lightships that protected shipping. The larger and heavier ships built for long voyages encountered shifting sands in the harbor, and navigation in and out of the "Great Harbor" became increasingly difficult. Eventually the harbor became blocked, in spite of rather ingenious methods of lifting the ships over the sandbar with "camels." It was a natural disaster.

In 1846 a devastating fire destroyed 36 acres of buildings, shops, homes and warehouses filled with oil. More than $1,000,000 in damage was done to the waterfront and surrounding areas. Hastily rebuilt, Nantucket changed catastrophically in appearance.

After 1850 the island population decreased by 1,000 every five years. In 1860 only six whaling vessels set sail, and the once-proud "banner town of the Commonwealth" was but a shadow of its former self. In 1869 the "bark Oak" set sail, never to return to port. The days of whaling were at an end.

In spite of its isolation and dwindling commercial life, the island continued to spend money to provide for its inhabitants. Citizens were allowed to work for the town in order to pay their taxes and, while times were hard, by the 1870s a new industry of tourism was beginning to appear.

A railroad was built to help with the influx, and the islanders who lived year-round began to rethink and rebuild their priorities. Scallops, once thought to be "nasty things," were harvested in the winter, and the fishing industry surged. Homes that once rented for $5 per month rented for $500 for the summer. The history, homes and lands were preserved, and Nantucket was reborn once more.

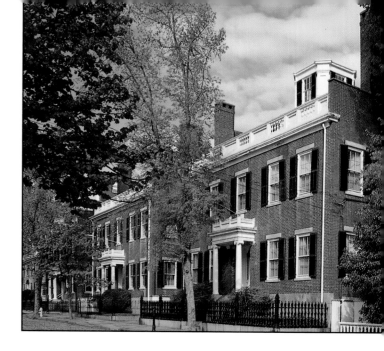

Above: View of "Three Bricks," built between 1836 and 1838 by Joseph Starbuck as gifts for his three sons.

Top right: Impressive entry to the house of Fredrick Mitchell, a wealthy whaling merchant who later became president of the Pacific Bank.

Below: The Athenaeum, the island's public library. It was designed by Frederick Coleman, who left his mark on the island's architecture in the 1840s.

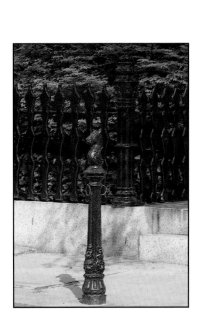

Right: Formal garden on Main Street.

Below: A shack, now quite out of place on Easy Street harbor.

A Beginning: The Lightship Era 1854 - 1905

The era of the lightship, from which the Nantucket lightship basket takes its name, was one of little glory and great loneliness. The function of these floating lighthouses was to warn captains of impending danger. But their roots can be traced back to Roman times. Marauding pirates in the eastern Mediterranean threatened coastal towns under the protection of Rome. Roman galleys, with fires burning in special baskets atop the masts, sailed the waters to give warning and to show approaching mariners the nearness of port. Their presence also told the mariners that the town was unplundered. As Rome declined, so too did the lightship.

Historically, the lightships were replaced by stationary lighthouses that marked coastlines and noted dangers. It wasn't until the lightship was revived, however, and stationed in the estuary of the Thames River in 1731, that the modern lightship was born.[9]

The lights of the *Nore*, the first lightship of the modern world, were two large lamps secured on spreaders extended from the yardarm. The lamps, which were useless in fog, were supplemented by a warning bell. Aside from the political problems of getting such ships commissioned, there were two major flaws: the ships would frequently break free from their moorings during heavy seas, and the flat wicks used in the warning lamps produced little light. Still, the ships' importance in navigation was considerable.

The United States government did not utilize lightships until 1819. This does not imply, however, that the government was cavalier about safe and accurate navigation. In fact, in 1786, Benjamin Franklin, the postmaster general of the United States whose mother was a Nantucket Folger, used Gulf Stream information created by Nantucket's Captain Timothy Folger to reduce sailing time to England by two weeks. Navigation and the charting of shoals and currents were essential to the safety and speed of shipping.

The largest and last commissioned Nantucket Lightship.

As commerce increased, demands for safer navigation became louder. Initially the United States government authorized two vessels to be commissioned and stationed in the Chesapeake Bay. The result must have been impressive, because in 1820 three additional vessels were authorized. The number of lightships grew to 30 by 1841, and duty on these lightships varied according to the station. "Outside" lightships were built to withstand the more severe elements of the sea. The anchors that held them in place were massive, yet still they failed in the heaviest of seas. The newer anchors were mushroom-shaped and totalled 7,800 pounds at the end of a 120-fathom chain. The first such "outside" lightship was anchored outside the entrance of New York Harbor.

As maritime traffic increased, the need for a lightship stationed off the south shoals of Nantucket island became obvious. While coastal lighthouses were being built as permanent nagivational aids, the dangerous shoals were woefully marked. Navigation through the busy sea lanes between Boston and New York, and the comings and goings of whaling vessels, created an unbelievable amount of traffic. It was estimated that as many as 500 vessels passed these shoals in 24 hours. Avoiding them meant a detour of hundreds of miles, while navigating them without any aids beyond charts could mean adding your ship to the countless number already lost at sea. Buoys were anchored during the more pleasant months of the year, yet it was during the rougher months that the real need for lightships was evident.

The shoals 20 miles southeast of the island of Nantucket were so treacherous that ships would frequently risk the dangers of the channels between Nantucket and the Vineyard instead. This passage was also fraught with danger, complicated by the constant shifting of sand moved by ocean currents. After numerous petitions to the government, the first Nantucket lightship was built in 1853, and painted red with a yellow mast[10]. The name *Nantucket South Shoal* was painted on the side of the 104-foot ship, which was anchored off the Davis South Shoal.

This ship was a far cry from the later vessels that were created with some thought for the comfort and safety of the crew during their long and lonely tour of duty. There seems to be little mention of the sacrifice that was endured by the women whose husbands and sons were part of the crew of any ship. The burden of running a home and attending to the finances fell on the shoulders of the women who were left at home. While the lightship created comparatively few widows, loneliness was not solely a male experience.

The *Nantucket South Shoal* was virtually destroyed when she was blown 50 miles off her mooring and dashed upon the rocks off Long Island. The terror of the crew can not be imagined as they floundered in a stormy winter sea. The crew was rescued, but this incident would be repeated 25 times by the replacement lightship, the *Nantucket New South Shoal No. 1*. Her tour of duty between 1855 and 1892 was both historic and heroic.

Eight-inch round Nantucket mould belonging to Stephen Gibbs. Courtesy of Douglas Porchette.

It was in 1856 that the first record of bringing moulds (blocks) on board to make baskets was recorded.[11] Life on the *South Shoal* lightship was described in *Century Magazine* in August of 1891. The ship was 103 feet long and 24 feet wide and was constructed of white and live oak with a two-hull construction. The inner side of the bulwarks was filled with salt to keep her "sweet." This process so toughened the wood that it was impervious to a bit and brace. The fore and aft masts were 71 feet high and at the 46-foot level round iron gratings served as day marks for others to sight the ship. The improved lanterns burned 900 gallons of oil a year. The lamps were lowered into lantern-houses which were built on deck around the masts. There, protected from the weather and waves, the lamps were cleaned, lighted and raised. The fog bell swung ten feet above the deck. It was noted in the *Century* article that the ship was rather indifferently outfitted to deal with the emergency of breaking free from her mooring.

A crew of ten people was responsible for the ordinary maintenance of the ship and its lights. Duties frequently involved manning the pumps to prevent the ship from being overwhelmed by the pounding sea. In the winter the ship was festooned with ice that hung from the rigging. The cold, ominous sea was ever present. The cabins were as roomy as possible and designed to prevent the occupant from being thrown from his bunk in heavy seas.

There was still the small library of books supplied by the Lighthouse Board, though the *South Shoal*'s crew "cannot be said to have made much use of the library." The only well-thumbed books described the disasters of ships lost on the Nantucket coast.

The crew was divided into two watches and they divided the work evenly. The lightship had its routine, which was prolonged in heavy weather. The duty was bleak, and the crew was paid only $600 for eight months. While hardly a handsome sum, the whole amount was kept intact. The government provided everything and there was nowhere to squander the money while at sea. Free time gave the crew and captain ample time to turn to handwork. Such activity was evident in the rope work that decorated railings and parts of the ship. Extra money was made with the production of baskets that were then sold in a number of stores on the islands. The baskets were sold individually or in "nests" of five or eight. It was said that the profit was so marginal that manufacture on the island never paid.[12] This reference clearly shows that the making of these baskets was not a lightship exclusive.

A few oblique mentions of rattan baskets give further evidence of the manufacture of these baskets prior to 1856. The making of the lightship baskets seemed to be more of an assembly process.[13] It was mentioned that the men produced the raw parts while on island during their leave. The watches spent a total of four months on island during the time between spring and winter. The two two-month periods enabled the crew to attend to the duties at home and to produce handwork necessary for the making of baskets. Such work was called "scrimshawing," a generic term that referred to the mechanical work.

The sizes of the baskets ranged from a pint to a peck and a half and were round or oval. They possessed lines of great beauty, and were also durable. Like the "bright-work" of the ship, these baskets were shellacked for durability and to aid in their maintenance. The lightship basket makers included William Appleton, Thomas Barrally, Oliver Coffin, Joseph Fisher, David and Davis Hall, Albert Hussey, Captain Thomas James, Captain David E. Ray, Sylvester Raymond, Captain Andrew Sandsbury, William Sandsbury, George Swain and Charles Sylvia. The name of Captain Charles B. Ray is associated with the production of 200 baskets by the year 1866.[14] The idea that he made 200 baskets on the lightship, however, is inaccurate. In fact, C. B. Ray was a whaleship master and never commanded a lightship. Clearly, many makers were producing these baskets on island and possibly during whaling voyages. While the article published in *Century* magazine stated otherwise, the making of these baskets must not have been so marginal as to have made them a lightship exclusive. The journal entry of Captain W. M. Davis stated "not enough to do to keep a man off a growl. I prefer to scrimshone." While Davis wasn't a basketmaker, it clearly shows that time was available for handwork, and the making of baskets was one option.

The name "lightship basket" is derived from the preponderance of basketmaking done on the ship. However, the use of this name is liberally applied to those baskets made on island. Actually, the baskets were all woven with rattan. The only exceptions might be a few examples constructed with palm leaf cut for weavers.

The year 1905 saw the end of service on the lightship by Nantucket islanders.[15] Technically, the era for the light-ship basket ended at that time. The word technically is used because most islanders saw the making of "authen-tic" lightship baskets to be the product of islanders only. The liberty comes with the label being applied to baskets made other than on the lightship. I have no doubt that the baskets continued to be made on the lightship and as such were of lightship origin.

There was a tale that lightship baskets ended because of a government-issued directive forbidding the making of baskets on the lightship. It appears that this informa-tion along with other folklore lacks fact, but does serve to perpetuate the mystique.

The baskets of more contemporary origins are referred to as Nantucket baskets. There are those who would say that one had to be an islander to make authentic Nantucket baskets. Perhaps that is why, in the 1940s, José Reyes initially called his baskets "friendship" baskets.[16] Although not from Nantucket, José Reyes is credited with reviving the tradition and popularity of Nantucket baskets. It should be noted that anyone born off Nantucket is never fully recognized as an islander. Some might feel these distinctions are splitting hairs, but the island has that prerogative, and while the origins and naming of these baskets may be somewhat clouded, the tradition is generational. The only clear distinction is the use of the word lightship. The lightship era came to an end when the government began to use electronic buoys. With the end of the era, the once proud fleet of 120 lightships was no more.

The decorative ropework shows the knotting techniques used by lightship sailors to pass the time.

The End of an Era, And a New Beginning 1940s - Present

Above: Covered round sewing basket made by José Reyes. Collection of Toni and Charles Frame.

A s with much of the history of the island, the manufacture of Nantucket baskets experienced a continual erosion in sales and suffered most severely during the Great Depression. The baskets were still made but the number of makers were fewer. Perhaps one of the more colorful characters was Clinton Mitchell ("Mitchy") Ray. Mitchy's father, Charles F. Ray, was a basketmaker as was his grandfather, Captain Charles B. Ray. Mitchy was responsible for the alteration of the poem about Nantucket baskets which now begins, "I was made on Nantucket. I'm strong and I'm stout, Don't lose me or burn me and I'll never wear out." His baskets were made of more traditional materials but varied greatly in quality. In pursuing the oral history about the makers of Nantucket baskets, I was told that his work improved when customers refused to accept his first effort.

Lauretta Gibbs, widow of Stephen Gibbs, a once prominent maker whose shop was located cn Madaket Road, told me that as a small boy her husband would take supper to Mitchy. Stephen's mother was a good cook and she made sure that Mitchy, who lived as a bachelor, was eating properly. Mitchy was a "bit of a character" and his neighbors looked after him. It was while delivering food that Gibbs was introduced to Nantucket baskets.

Left: Note the ivory pins, buttons and double whale decoration in this small antique oval evening bag. Collection of Toni and Charles Frame. Made by José Reyes.

Right: Round, low-sided Nantucket with heart handles, made by "Mitchy" Ray. Collection of Douglas Porchette.

"Mitchy" Ray holding one of his baskets.
Courtesy Douglas Porchette.

Mrs. Gibbs was quick to point out that prior to his work with baskets her husband was an accomplished woodworker and a builder on the island. It was when he suffered a heart attack that he turned to basketmaking. "Much of what he did he learned on his own," Mrs. Gibbs said, "and the people who bought his work were buying quality. I did all the weaving and he did the rest. While José was perhaps better known, my husband's work was superior."

A nephew, Douglas Porchette, spent his summers on the island helping and told me that they had a Reyes' basket in the shop for comparison. When asked why her husband's work was more expensive, Mrs. Gibbs explained the quality found in a Gibbs' basket by flexing José's basket. As the cane ribs yielded, she said, customers usually got the idea.

"They were always two years behind in orders," said Doug. "I spent time working on correspondence, making baskets and helping around the guest house that they ran to make their living. They never advertised because they couldn't make them any faster and they had enough business."

Doug added that the baskets were sold by a number which referred to a specific size. He also stated that his Uncle Steve said that "you could have heated your house for a long time on the weaving blocks that were thrown out at the Madaket dump."

I asked Mrs. Gibbs if there was anything else she wished to add in the interview. She choked up: "We were honorable people and sold our work for far less than the prices of today. We did what was required to make ends meet." Her memory, she said, "wasn't as clear as it once was," nor was her sight, but her gentle recall added a human dimension to the baskets that were made in that time. She stated that her husband had made baskets for 20 years and had been gone for 16, but his work was still admired. I can attest to that, because the owners I talked to were proud of their Gibbs' baskets. Today, the making of Nantucket baskets is seeing a Renaissance. The summer trade, which has been the principal market, is offered baskets of every shape, size and origin. The penetration of the market by Oriental "copies" now confuses the buyers and complicates the marketing of these woven treasures.

The shape of this covered oval basket with its braided leather strap and ebony decoration is unusual with front corners cut at a 45-degree angle on a rectangular base. Made by José Reyes. Collection of the Nantucket Historical Association.

The most recognized form of the basket is the covered oval purse. Thought to be antique in origin, it is instead a contemporary twist. José Reyes conceived of the form in about 1948, and the addition of a carved ebony whale by Charles Sayle finished the look.

Today the shapes vary with the maker and the prices vary just as much. I must confess that $3,200 for what was admittedly a spectacular example shocked me, but the customers have a wide range of qualities and prices from which to select their price—or the option of making it themselves.

NOTES

1. Robert Gambee, *Nantucket Island* (New York: W. W. Norton and Company, 1986), 137.

2. Alexander Starbuck, *The History of Nantucket* (Boston: C. E. Goodspeed and Company, 1924), 16-17.

3. William Root Bliss, *Quaint Nantucket* (Boston: Houghton Mifflin Company, 1896).

4. Alexander Starbuck, *The History of Nantucket*.

5. Mary Elizabeth Starbuck, *My House and I* (Boston: Houghton Mifflin Company, 1929), 258-259.

6. Richard Kugler, *The Whale Oil Trade 1750-1775* (New Bedford: Old Dartmouth Historical Society, 1980).

7. Proceedings from the Pacific National Bank, Nantucket, Mass.

8. Nantucket Historical Association Collection, *Nantucket Friends Records: Births, Deaths, Received, Disowned, Restored 1711-1838.* (Nantucket: NHA Collection 52, Box 6, Folder 6A)

9. Frederick L. Thompson, *The Lightships of Cape Cod* (Maine: Congress Square Press, 1983), 35.

10. Ibid., 35.

11. Charles H. and Mary Grace Carpenter, *The Decorative Arts and Crafts of Nantucket* (New York: Dodd, Mead, and Company, 1978), 185.

12. Thompson, *The Lightships of Cape Cod*, 109.

13. Gustav Kobbe, "Life on the South Shoal Lightship," *The Century Magazine*, 1891.

14. Everett U. Crosby, *Books and Baskets, Signs and Silver of Old-Time Nantucket* (printed privately, 1940), 68.

15. Grace Brown Gardner, *Scrapbook* (Nantucket Historical Association Collection), vol. 9.

16. José Formosa Reyes, *The Friendship Baskets and Their Maker, José Formosa Reyes* (Brochure, Nantucket, Mass., 1960).

ANTIQUE BASKETS

Baskets are becoming some of the most sought-after collectibles in the antique marketplace, according to auctioneers, antique dealers and collectors. Consequently, prices have increased dramatically over the years due to heightened interest and the search for "affordable" examples. One of the most desirable forms has always been the Nantucket basket. These woven treasures are appreciated not only for the functions they serve, but for their restrained beauty. While Nantucket baskets are never inexpensive, their rapidly escalating prices require the general public to become more knowledgeable about them. This information is useful to both the seller and the buyer.

There is an art to viewing baskets. It is acquired with experience and heightened by awareness. Knowing what to look for in a well-made basket will prevent costly errors and insure pride of ownership. Naturally, budgetary considerations affect any purchase, but one good basket is always a better investment than many inferior ones. This is especially true when you are selling a collection. Understanding how a basket is made will allow you to recognize flaws and deficiencies in a maker's work. These baskets are presented as inspirations to the collector, dealer and maker. Study them carefully. Learn how to judge a basket and how to care for it. I hope that my reflections will enable you to analyze a basket, be it antique or contemporary, making you a more informed and appreciative collector, dealer or maker.

Top left: Oval Nantucket basket made by A. D. Williams. Collection of the Nantucket Historical Association.

Top right: Covered round Nantucket basket made by John Brown Folger. Collection of the Nantucket Historical Association.

Left: The swing-handle treatment on this Indian basket reflects the influence of the Nantucket basket handle on wood-splint basket construction.

Right: Antique oval moulds belonging to Stephen Gibbs. Courtesy of Douglas Porchette.

The Round Nantucket

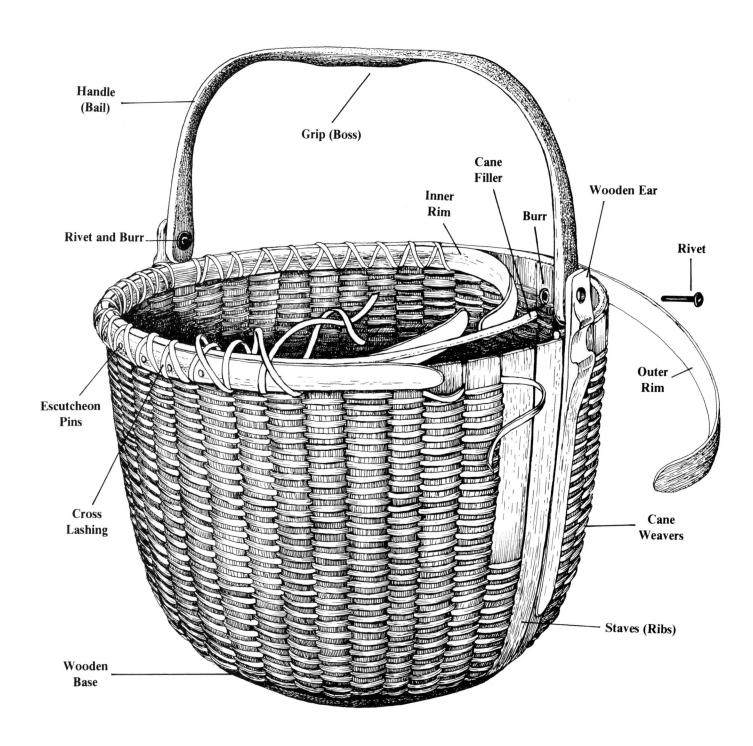

Handle
(Bail)

Grip (Boss)

Cane
Filler

Inner
Rim

Wooden Ear

Burr

Rivet

Rivet and Burr

Escutcheon
Pins

Outer
Rim

Cross
Lashing

Cane
Weavers

Staves (Ribs)

Wooden
Base

The Oval Nantucket

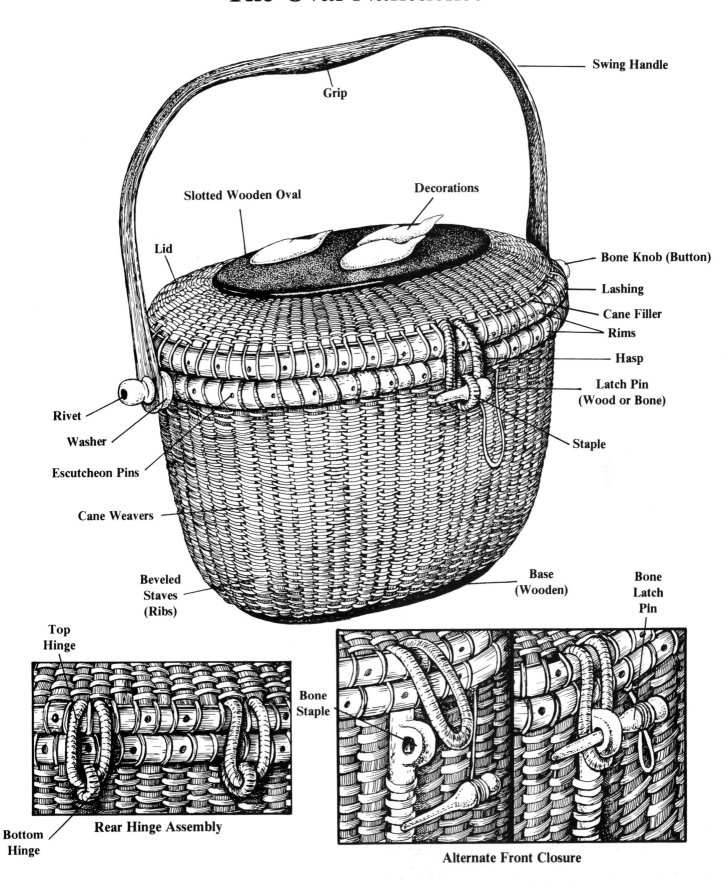

Swing Handle

Grip

Slotted Wooden Oval

Decorations

Lid

Bone Knob (Button)

Lashing

Cane Filler

Rims

Hasp

Latch Pin
(Wood or Bone)

Rivet

Washer

Staple

Escutcheon Pins

Cane Weavers

Beveled
Staves
(Ribs)

Base
(Wooden)

Bone
Latch
Pin

Top
Hinge

Bottom
Hinge

Rear Hinge Assembly

Bone
Staple

Alternate Front Closure

Judging Antique Baskets

The judging of a basket from the perspective of maker, seller or buyer is extremely important. It is imperative in the purchasing of antique baskets that a number of factors be considered. These factors can then be transposed to new baskets. The first and perhaps the most important aspect is the "look" of the basket. The overall appearance of the basket should be one of a whole. No one feature of any basket should stand out above the other. If your eye is drawn to a part, it is possibly out of proportion. The shape as a whole should be pleasing to the eye and the side of the basket should taper slightly for appearance and removal from the block by the maker.

The next element is the material. The better baskets are constructed using wooden uprights, rims and handles. The use of brass ears versus wooden can be a functional, aesthetic and historical consideration. Earlier baskets used wooden ears; the use of metal appeared in the 1860s. The quality of the cane and its weaving width are also important.

The sizes of cane were not as varied as today, and the width sold presently as "narrow medium" was heavily used. Larger sizes of cane were available for the more massive baskets, and some makers graduated weavers from finer to wider widths to improve appearance. The color of the cane should be darkened with age and the weavers, if delicately shifted, should reveal a lighter protected area on the upright. Chemical agents such as potassium permanganate can synthetically age a basket, but tend to collect in recesses and should be visible with careful examination. The cane should vary in color due to the variations found naturally on the inner bark of the rattan vine. The weaving should be even and uniform. The unsightly bulges which result when cane is not scarf-joined should not be present.

Top: A close-up view of a handle and metal ear assembly on a large Nantucket basket. Collection of the author.

Bottom: A close-up of the handle detail on a New Hampshire farm basket, showing the riveted handle treatment.

The uprights, or ribs (staves, spokes), should be finely prepared. Ribs of the earlier baskets seem to be predominantly oak and hickory. The ribs should be smooth, uniform, in proportion to the size of the basket and beveled on the outer edges. The ribs should narrow gracefully at one end, allowing insertions into the grooved base, and should be aligned closely together to allow for the weaving. The ribs should be on a direct line to the center of the base and should not drift in appearance once woven. They should also show a monotony of grain. This appearance would show the understanding of grain and growth rings by the maker and add to the strength of the basket.

Ribs showing grain patterns and an unusual choice of wood are more likely machined and contemporary. While visually attractive, these can be weaker and can tend to complicate the weaving process due to potential breaking. Wood prepared properly should not require the molding of the ribs to the block.

Interior view of an antique Nantucket Basket. Note the alignment of spokes to the base and the decorative turnings in the bottom. Collection of Charles and Barbara Adams.

The bottom of the basket is a critical element. A number of features are evident in the best baskets. The thickness of the base should be in proportion to the size of the basket. It appears that the choice of 7/16" was widely used. The wood varied according to what was available, with pine appearing to be a last resort and the more stable hardwoods the wood of choice. The choice of exotic or specially figured woods probably indicates a contemporary origin. Decorative rings cut into the bottom of the basket were simply that, and while designs were repetitively used, they were not necessarily the signature of the maker.

A round basket sold as old should not have a perfectly round bottom. Wood shrinks unevenly, and a perfectly round base indicates that the time necessary to qualify the basket as old has not graced that particular object.

The inside edge of the bottom should be gracefully arced. The underneath edge should be beveled or undercut to give a graceful line to the base. Cumbersome bases should be a clue to a poor basket. The diameter of the bottom should be pleasing to the eye. The proportion of a five-inch bottom to an eight-inch basket would seem correct.

Contemporary rims are more likely reed, and seldom larger than a half-inch in width. Rims on older baskets were wooden and, again, showed understanding and concern for the integal strength of the basket. Talented makers understood the natural proclivity of wood,

especially unseasoned wood, to bend in certain directions. The grain pattern, when correctly utilized, enabled the maker to form proportional yet strong rims.

This understanding of green wood allowed the makers to form "heart handles" that were incredibly delicate and understated. The larger side handles of today are necessary to permit the maker to use seasoned woods. The more substantial size, too, greatly increases the success ratio of bending these boiled or steamed handles. A fairly safe rule is, the larger the heart (side) handles, the later the basket.

A close-up view showing the beginning and ending of lashing on the exterior of a Boyer basket. Collection of Olive Hubbard.

Above: Open Nantucket tray with heart handles. Made by José Reyes. Collection of Toni and Charles Frame.

Right: A finely woven low-sided Nantucket basket with heart handles. Made by Captain James Weyer. Collection of the Nantucket Historical Association.

Opposite page, top left: Interior of handle, ear and lashing detail of a Boyer basket. Collection of Olive Hubbard.
Top right: Detail of handle and ear construction. Collection of the Nantucket Historical Association.
Bottom left: Handle detail of J. B. Folger lidded round Nantucket basket. Collection of the Nantucket Historical Association.
Bottom right: Interior of handle and rim detail of a Weyer basket. Collection of the Nantucket Historical Association.

Below left: Details of carved ivory decorations, with ebony (top), with rosewood (center) and all ivory (bottom). Collection of the Nantucket Historical Association.
Below right: Oval Nantucket with cover, made by José Reyes. Note the ebony buttons, pin and top with three ivory whales made by Althea Macy. Collection of the Nantucket Historical Association.

Handle lengths for the bail handle of a Nantucket vary according to the maker. The shortest handles were one-half the circumference of the basket. The longest used this "one-half circumference" and added two inches. This proportion allowed the handles to nest inside one another and rest on the rim of the basket.

The newer version of the Nantucket basket is the covered oval purse. Except for the handle, many of the same rules apply, as they would with any basket. The real concern is not to get caught up in folklore and lose sight of the quality. An abundant use of ivory may very well escalate the cost and cloud the quality. I personally feel the use of ivory hardly qualifies the basket as more historic, because the utilization of ivory is a contemporary addition. While laws are in place in this country to

"protect" the elephant, the use of ivory sets into motion the supply and demand cycle, and elephants are poached as a result. The use of kangaroo and camel bone is a popular substitute, and fossilized ivory is fairly plentiful.

A good-quality purse has all the proportional features of the oval or round. The base size is not so great as to prevent a graceful arc from the bottom as it integrates with the side. The top is also pleasant and the number of ribs should be mirrored in the top. Often more ribs are placed in the top to increase the appearance of fineness. Don't let a spectacular top alone sell you on a basket.

Left: Deep Nantucket covered oval with ivory pin and ebony and ivory top. Note the absence of ivory buttons on handle. Made by José Reyes. Collection of Toni and Charles Frame.
Below: Covered Nantucket purse with ivory buttons, pin and seagull decoration. Made by José Reyes. Collection of Toni and Charles Frame.

The hinge placement and size of leather wrapped with cane should be pleasant and unobtrusive. The composition of the hinges and closures should give you a clue as to quality. Plastic shoelaces or similar materials are used in the cheap copies. Handles should be carved wood, not the porous rattan found on the inexpensive foreign versions. The handles are higher than proportional to allow the basket to be comfortable on the arm and to swing out of the way of the lid.

The escutcheon pins that are part of the rim construction are small, and are clipped before they are hammered round on the cut end to prevent their working free. Unsightly, folded-over nails show a disregard for appearance and should be avoided. Further stabilizing of the rims comes with the lashing, done with the same cane width as the basket. Purses are frequently woven from fine cane to improve the overall appearance. Four- to five-millimeter binder cane is used to fill the void between the two rims. On a better example, a fine cane is lashed under the exposed rim to conceal the area where the rim connects with the uprights.

Detail of rear hinge treatment. Note the simple hinge treatment and decorative wrapping. Collection of the Nantucket Historical Association.

Above left: Classic Boyer ten-inch round Nantucket basket with metal ear treatment. Collection of Olive Hubbard.

Above right: Miniature round Nantucket basket. Collection of Toni and Charles Frame.

Left: Round Nantucket basket signed by Sprague. Collection of the Nantucket Historical Association.

Single or double lashing is an artistic prerogative and has nothing to do with valuation. The only exception would be when double lashing dominates the appearance of the rim and detracts from the look. The lashing should be neat and uniform.

The last elements are the finish and the maker's label. Obviously, a well-finished basket with a patina still intact is the best. The earlier finishes are frequently worn to a mellow glow. The earliest finish was likely shellac, and the later varnish; however, they are hard to distinguish. The interior should show the lightest evidence of finishing to allow the basket to breathe. Outside finishes are denser, but they by no means obliterate the grain of the woods or plasticize the appearance of the basket. Polyurethane finishes lack a warmth of character and are frequently applied so liberally that they ruin the look.

Naturally, signed or paper labeled baskets are usually worth more than unsigned. However, a poorly made, labeled basket hardly rivals a finer unlabeled antique.

Right: Bottom view of signed Boyer basket with a label containing a famous poem extolling the strength of the Nantucket basket. Collection of Olive Hubbard.

Bottom left: O. C. Coffin label for an oval Nantucket basket. Collection of Charles and Barbara Adams.

Below right: Close-up view of David F. Ray's label showing the $2.00 price on a nine-inch basket. Collection of Olive Hubbard.

I WAS MADE
ON NANTUCKET ISLAND
I AM STRONG AND STOUT
DON'T LOSE OR BURN ME
I'LL NEVER WEAR OUT

MADE BY S. P. BOYER

MANUFACTURED BY
O. C. COFFIN,
FORMERLY OF
South Shoal Lightship.

MANUFACTURED BY
DAVID E. RAY,
On board the
SOUTH SHOAL LIGHTSHIP.

Above: Low round Nantucket basket. Collection of the Nantucket Historical Association.

Right: Oval Nantucket basket with metal ears and swing handle. Labeled "Manufactured by O. C. Coffin, formerly of the South Shoal Lightship."

Caring For A Treasure

The first rule is to keep your baskets out of excessive heat or climatic conditions. Periodically clean dust and grime from the basket carefully. Dust can be blown out of the bottom and sides using compressed air such as is containerized for cleaning delicate photographic lenses. The blower end of a vacuum can be carefully used. Some dry brushing with a fine hair paintbrush can loosen dirt. A mixture of polyethelene glycol (PEG) and water, lightly dampened onto

a bristle paint brush, can also help in the cleaning. Dirt and our polluted atmosphere produce a mildly sulphuric acid which is harmful. Washing a basket can be disastrous. And if you handle your baskets a great deal, wear cotton gloves. Over time, the oil from your skin will darken the basket.

No new finishes should be applied. Alcohol concoctions using glycerine can produce a greasy film that attracts dirt. Furniture polishes should be avoided, especially those with a propellant since they tend to cloud finishes. A fine paste wax should be carefully applied to the exposed wooden parts of a new basket, and then buffed to a luster. Remember that baskets are wood and can be invaded by powder post beetles. Extermination is necessary should wood dust and small holes appear. Ivory should be protected when not in "use."

This maintenance cycle for new baskets should be a monthly one. Once again, paste wax is recommended; however, caution in waxing should be used to prevent the wax from involving the weaving. The hinges should be oiled at least twice a year and only the best oil should be used. The leather is an organic material and the maintenance of these hinges will prevent costly repairs.

Speaking of repairs, they are not easily accomplished. While you may know how to make a basket, you probably won't often find yourself repairing one you made. The condition and age of the materials composing a basket greatly affect the ability to repair it. If you think this is an easy way to make some extra cash, think again. Further damage to a basket can lead to a lawsuit. Customers need to know and acknowledge their willingness to take the risks included with a repair. Coloring cane with aniline dyes and finishes requires experience. Think twice before you offer to fix a basket and remember that it will take twice the time for a repair. Remember, too, that years of experience are helpful.

One final note. The marketplace has been invaded by a number of foreign versions. These reproductions are characterized by a disregard for finished appearance on the inside, especially at the rims. The handles are usually made of reed and lack character. The hinges, if wrapped at all, are likely to be plastic or plastic-coated material. The bases and tops are poorly shaped, sanded and finished. Frequently, good scrimshaw is used to camouflage deficiencies. Antiqued looks can be relatively easily faked. Become an educated consumer and you can save yourself a great deal of money. If you are in doubt about any aspect of a basket, consult an expert. The expense is better than the regret.

Woodworking Fundamentals

The making of baskets is now and has always been a work of individual expression. No single approach is correct. I have developed the techniques presented in the following pages in an attempt to minimize the necessary number of tools, and feel they most reasonably represent an approach to making "Nantuckets" appropriate to the heyday of their manufacture. Some of the steps can be eliminated by purchasing the parts that are difficult to make, but the whole process is explained for those who wish to understand the entire method. In the section involving the use of power tools I have condensed some information, and suggest that if you are not experienced in their use you do not attempt these steps without adequate supervision or further instruction. Safety is essential, and every precaution should be taken to prevent personal injury.

Tools and Materials

Essential Tools

Knife

Tape measure

Scissors

Spring clamps or clothespins

Small awl or screwdriver

Sandpaper

Small paintbrush

Small drill bits and drill

Piece of leather to cover
    your knee

Wire cutter

Hammer

Piece of heavy metal or anvil

Small saw

Wood rasp to shape base

Drawknife

Froe and mallet

Optional Tools

Lathe and turning tools

Safety goggles

Shavehorse

Materials

Mould (block)

Wood 7/16″ hardwood

Staves (wood, cane or reed)

Material for a rim (reed or wood)

Escutcheon pins

Precarved handle with brass ear
    or wood for this project

Cane

Rivets and burrs

Finish for basket

A variety of lumber, including teak, cherry and curly maple, can be used to make bases for the Nantucket basket.

Right: Different woods and synthetics can be turned as bases. The white base is DuPont Corian, which can be carved and turned.

Below: Nesting set of oval contemporary Nantucket moulds. Collection of the author.

Inset: Antique Nantucket round mould. Collection of the author.

Moulds are critical elements in the making of Nantucket baskets. While shapes vary according to the makers, the baskets graduate in sizes to allow them to "nest." Individually crafted, moulds may take the form of solid blocks, hollow blocks or inventive collapsible shapes which allow for the basket's easy removal. Most moulds have (or accept) a threaded bolt inserted in the form which allows the maker to secure the base (and thus the basket) while weaving. Antique blocks are quite scarce today.

51

Creating a Base for the Round Nantucket

In our projects we are using 7/16″ cherry lumber, milled to that thickness by a lumberyard or specialty lumber supplier. Such thickness appears to be used for baskets up to 12″ in diameter. Miniatures will obviously use thinner stock.

The standard formula is a 5″ base for an 8″ basket. This proportion supplies the ratio for calculating bases. Since we are making a 9″ basket, our base calculates to 5-5/8″. Using a compass, set it at half the 5-5/8″ diameter, or 2-13/16″. Embed the point of the compass to clearly mark the center, and strike the circle.

Drill a 3/16″ hole in the center (already marked by the compass). Carefully position the drill vertically, using a brad point drill to help center the bit. A drill press insures a vertical bore but is unnecessary. Advance through the board slowly to avoid splintering the wood. This hole size will allow you to use a standard dowel to plug the hole when the basket is finished. A white plastic knitting needle will also fill the hole and will even simulate ivory.

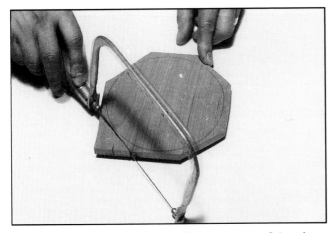

Use a saw to cut off the corners of the piece of wood used. This eliminates some waste prior to the actual turning of the base. It is not necessary to precut a circle.

Mount the base blank on a screw center or a center that has been modified to accept a threaded 3/16″ rod.

Creating a Base for the Round Nantucket

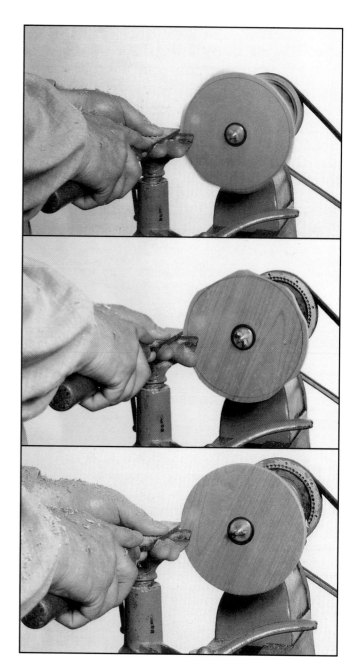

These views show the mounted base flush to the surface of the center. Now buffer the base with a rubber or leather washer and tighten the base to the center, using a metal washer and wing nut.

Before you start to work on the lathe, remember these safety measures: Wear safety goggles. Tie your hair back. Remove all jewelry and loose clothing. And never position any cutting tool against the material to be shaped and then turn the machine on.

Secure the tapered end of the screw center into the headstock of the lathe. Position the toolrest slightly below the center and parallel to the base, allowing a small clearance. Use the slowest speed position on the lathe's belt adjustment. Use a skew to round the bottom. Position the tool so that the skew can be slid easily between the first finger (placed against the toolrest) and the thumb that holds the tool against the rest. Gradually advance the skew through the outermost waste. Repeat this process using the straight edge of the tool as a vertical reference to cut the edge at a 90-degree angle. Continue to slowly remove the waste until the pencil line of the circle is carefully removed and the base is fully round. At this point you might check the base to the mould (block) for a proper fit.

While the lathe is turning, mark a center line on the cut vertical edge. This is the cutting line for the slotting chisel that makes the 1/2″ deep groove for the ribs. A saw can be used to create this groove independently of the lathe.

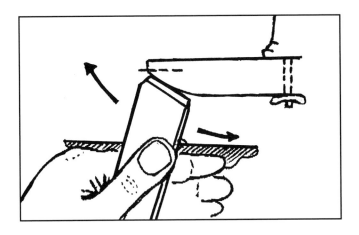

Reposition the parallel toolrest to allow for better access to the surface being worked. Use the full cutting surface of the skew to shape the edge of the disk. The top edge is saucer shaped and the cutting action is stopped short of the pencil line for the slot.

Continue to use the skew with its flat surface in contact with the toolrest, and cut in an arc motion. The lighter surface on the edge shows the shaped area. With the chisel in the same position, create decorative lines by slowly pressing the corner of the skew into the cherry or other hardwood. Make the lines deep enough so they will not be sanded away.

Use a gouge with the profile of the decorations you wish to create. Slowly advance the gouge, which is held firmly against the toolrest. You may arc the tool to widen the groove, but NEVER LIFT A TOOL OFF THE TOOLREST AND ATTEMPT ANYTHING IN MIDAIR. Make as many rings as you wish, but avoid deep cut grooves near the rounded edge. Be careful not to hit the wing nut with your tool.

Creating a Base for the Round Nantucket

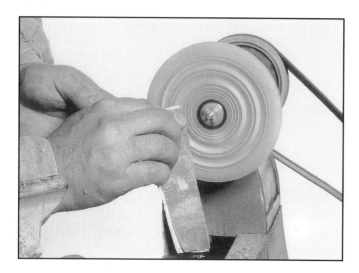

Remove the toolrest. While the base is turning, sand the features of the base. Be sure to insulate your fingers from the heat created by the friction by using several folds of sandpaper. The final polishing of the base can be done using a handful of wood shavings or a soft scouring pad.

To create the slot in the base, use a slotting chisel (customized parting chisel) that has been hollow ground to prevent binding. The width of the cut is about the thickness of a hacksaw blade. Reposition the toolrest to be parallel with the edge of the base and close to the work area. Slowly push the firmly anchored chisel into the pencil line

created to mark the slot. As you advance the cut, hesitate periodically to let the tool cool. While the base is rotating, clean out the slot with a piece of sandpaper. A slotting saw can be purchased to use in a drillpress to create the same result. You can also hand cut this groove with a saw.

The foot, or back edge, is created by using either a gouge or the skew. A 45-degree angle is cut to improve the profile of the base. The gouge will create a concave radius.

Making a Wooden Knob for the Covered Round

Use a small 1-1/2" square of a hardwood (maple in our case) and remove the corners so as to facilitate the turning process. Drill the center with a tap hole which allows the block to be turned onto a screw center.

Secure the taper into the headstock and seat it with a slight blow of a hammer. Position the toolrest slightly below center, parallel to the longitudinal axis and close to the material, allowing the wood to turn freely. Using a gouge or round nose chisel, slowly turn the octagonal piece of wood round by carefully removing the waste. The process is accomplished by sliding the cutting tool up and down the toolrest and removing small bits of material at a time. The toolrest edge can be used to help sight the uniformity of the cylinder being created. Remember to hold the tools securely in position against the toolrest.

The knob is created by using a chisel that allows you to create a nub (stud) in the center of the top. The stud is then undercut using a parting chisel to create the knob. The disc of wood below the knob is shaped to create a gentle slope to the edge and can be decorated much like the round bottom.

Making a Wooden Knob for the Covered Round

Carefully refine the appearance of your turning prior to sanding. A light touch with your cutting tools is essential.

Sand the parts smooth. Be sure to move the toolrest to gain safe and easy access to your work.

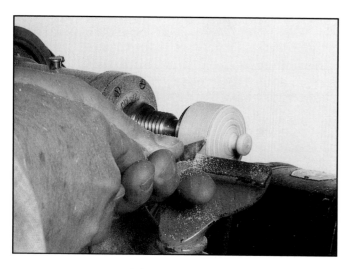

Reposition the toolrest. Cut a groove into the knob about 1/2″ deep and the same thickness of the groove cut into the bottom. The thickness of the knob and its base can vary. Antique examples are delicate and understated.

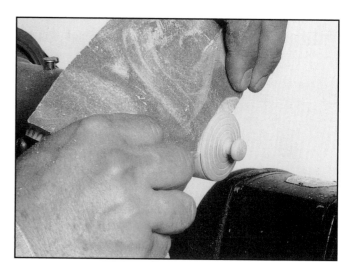

Sand the groove to clean and widen it if necessary. Remember, when sanding, move the toolrest out of the way.

Reposition the toolrest parallel to the axis. Leave about 3/16″ of wood beyond the groove and generously undercut the entire knob. Before the knob is too weakened, turn a foot on the base similar to that found on the bottom.

Widen-out the undercutting so the parting chisel doesn't bind.

These views show an alternative that can be made by creating a small turned bottom (disc) and then filling the turning hole with a Shaker style knob carved to fit.

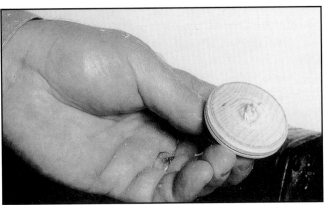

The final cutoff is done while firmly holding the parting chisel against the toolrest. Get ready to catch the knob as you push the chisel through the remaining nub of wood. Any excess can be sanded off.

Creating an Oval Base with String

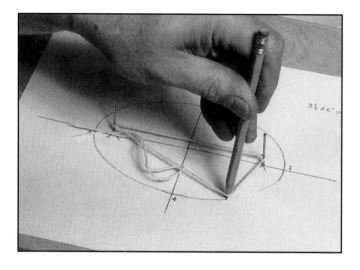

This view shows how to draw an oval using a string, three nails, a compass and a piece of paper.

1. Select your base size. For this example, I have decided upon a 3-1/2" x 6" oval.

2. Draw a horizontal line and bisect it with a vertical axis. Number the right horizontal line #1, the top vertical #2, the left horizontal line #3 and the bottom vertical #4.

3. Set your compass at 1-3/4" and position it in the center. Mark your measurement on lines #2 and #4.

4. Set your compass at 3" and place it on the center of the intersection. Mark your measurement on lines #1 and #4.

5. Using the 3" setting, place the compass at the marks on lines #2 and #4 and intersect the horizontal axis.

6. Drive nails at the intersection points on the horizontal axis and at the mark on line #4.

7. Tie a tight string around the three points, thus creating a triangle.

8. Remove the nail on line #4 and position a sharp lead pencil on the inside of the string. Stretch the string taut and move the pencil against the string, marking the oval pattern on the paper. Transfer the pattern to a 7/16" thick piece of wood.

9. Cut out the wooden oval pattern, round its edges with a wood rasp, sand it smooth, and saw a groove for the ribs.

Find a piece of thin wood that will allow you to raise a saw to the proper height for slotting the base in the center, and cut a 1/2" deep groove around the base. In this photo is a commercially available slotting saw that is used in a drill press. As with all tools, get help when you first attempt anything.

Riving Oak for the Staves (Spokes, Ribs, Uprights)

It appears that most early Nantucket baskets were constructed with oak staves. The process of riving, or splitting out, the oak staves insures the stability and integrity of the basket. Sawn staves can be created without regard for the growth pattern of the wood used, but they tend to split or crack more easily. Many makers use reed, veneered wood, ash (either pounded or cut) or wide binder cane. I have even seen examples using recut tongue depressors or wooden coffee stirs.

The technique for splitting any wood is the same. The first rule is to split the tree from the top toward the bottom. To determine the top, examine the growth rings, which are thinner at the top than at the bottom. Quarter the tree and then rehalve your quarters. Remove the dark heartwood from the lighter sapwood by using a froe and mallet. Strike the froe on the top edge, driving the sharpened blade between the junction of the heartwood/sapwood. Then twist it carefully from side to side down the length of the wood.

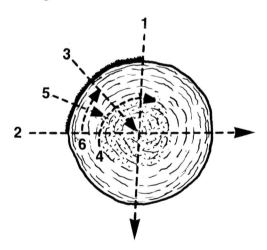

Remove the bark. Then, using a froe, alternately split the wood either across the growth rings or with them. The rule is, always split your stock in halves. Stop dividing across the growth rings when the billet of wood is about 1″ wide with the growth rings stacked on top of each other.

In these pictures I chose to use a short piece of white oak for demonstration. A longer piece of wood would reduce the amount of duplication. Caution: White oak will gray in color when held in water too long. If you wish to keep oak fresh after splitting out stock, wrap pieces in freezer paper and place in freezer. Thaw to use.

Riving Oak for the Staves (Spokes, Ribs, Uprights)

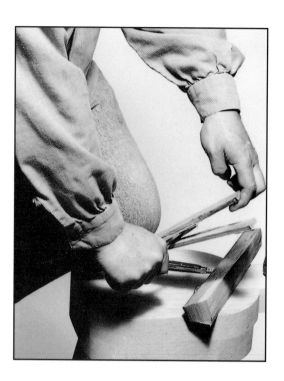

Should your division run off (become uneven), apply greater pressure and pull on the heavier side while SLOWLY continuing your split, and the correction should take place. Body language will help add pressure.

Final divisions are always accomplished by continuously halving the wood using the growth ring pattern as your splitting marks. This finer subdivision can be done with a sturdy-bladed knife.

Continue to halve the wood until you are down to the desired thickness. Heavier single rings can be subdivided, scraped or sanded thinner.

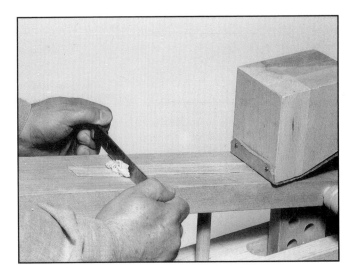

Hold your knife stationary, and use a leather covering on your thigh to allow you to slide the wood into the blade. Hold your knife nearly parallel to the surface of the wood, and scrape the wood smooth on both sides. A final vertical scraping with the knife will further polish the surface.

You can use your drawknife and shavehorse or a shaving beam made from a cut-down sawhorse for this process. The blade of the drawknife can be used in a vertical position to scrape the wood smooth. You may elect to use a sharp paint scraper.

This photo shows bark patterns of white ash (left) and black ash (right). Both woods, when fresh, can be pounded out using a wooden mallet or hammer. The delaminated piece in the center shows how the growth rings are released. Historically white oak was commonly used; however, ash is easier to prepare.

Stave Patterns

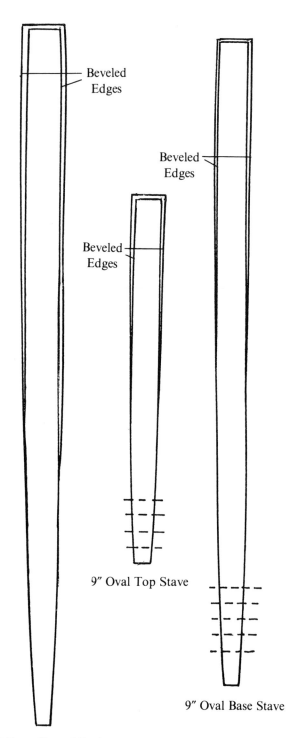

Beveled Edges

Beveled Edges

Beveled Edges

9″ Oval Top Stave

9″ Oval Base Stave

9″ Stave Round Basket

Making a Stave

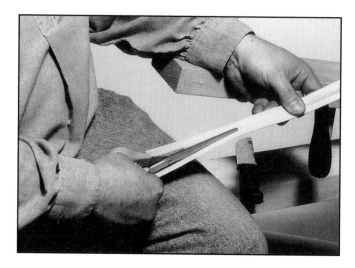

Since we are making a 9″ round basket, the staves are going to be about 1/2″ wide. This width is either reduced or increased according to the size of the basket. Straighten the left edge of the 1″ cleaned material and cut it down the middle. Then straighten the outer edge to create two 1/2″ uniform staves.

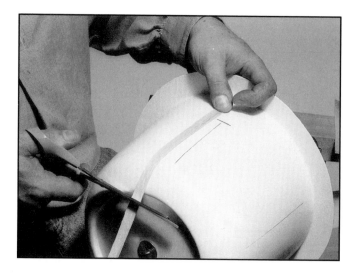

The length you need to cut your staves for this basket is approximately 7″. The uprights insert into the base and will be about 1″ longer than the finished height of the woven basket. Old moulds have scored lines indicating varying weaving heights of baskets.

Our newer plastic version has an indentation for the correct weaving height of 5-3/4″ (highlighted with a permanent marker), and I will add vertical reference marks to alert me that my staves are drifting out of alignment when I am weaving.

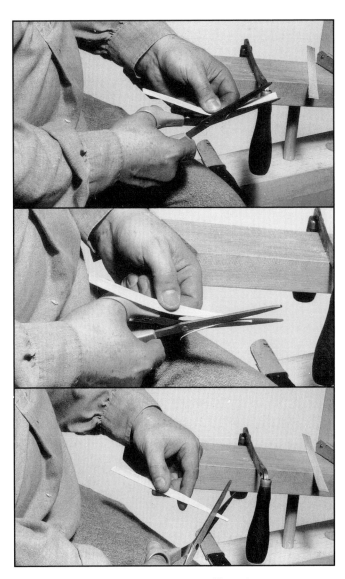

The 9″ basket usually uses either 49 or 51 staves if they are about 1/2″ wide at the top. When in doubt, fewer are better. The stave thickness is between 1/32″ and 1/16″.

A stave for a round basket tapers uniformly, with the tapered edge cut on a gradual rounded curve toward the tip. The taper is 4″ long and the width of the stave at the end is reduced to about 1/4″ when finished. The shaping of staves for proper weaving appearance is an aesthetic judgment that takes practice to achieve. Once again, these dimensions are for a 9″ basket and will require a proportional increase or decrease for other sizes. Should you find your taper is a bit too pointed, clip off a small portion of the end.

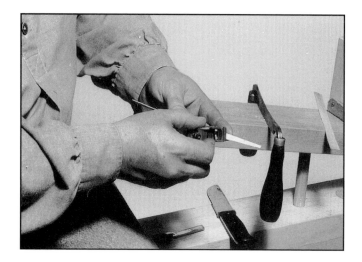

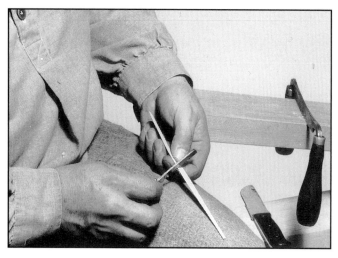

If the staves are beveled on the outer edge, the cane will lie closer and improve the overall appearance. The convex curve of the staves should be placed to the outside, allowing the natural bend of the wood to help in the weaving appearance. Some people use a belt sander to shape the staves, but this is rather tricky. I use a small plane, a knife or sandpaper.

Tips on Shaping Purse Staves

The finer staves, or spokes, for the 9″ purse are 3/8″ to 1/4″ and tapered proportionally, like any rib. Because of the sharp radii at the ends of the oval, more staves are needed to fill the ends properly. If you shape all staves the same, you can cut off the narrowed ends to allow for proper fitting as you approach the more gradual curves of the oval. The centerpoint of the oval should have staves with the least taper. I suggest you cut your staves for the purse at least 1-1/2″ longer than anticipated to allow for this customization.

Important: Before you weave your basket, press or tie your staves against the mould to check alignment. Once your look is correct, you can mark your mould to note positioning and number of staves for future baskets.

If you are using wide binder cane for the staves, a formula can help in determining the number to cut. Measure the top of the mould in centimeters. Add a zero to that number and divide by eight. This will give you the number of staves (for example, 55 + 0 = 550 divided by 8 = 68.75 or 69 staves).

Nesting set of round Nantucket baskets made by Captain James Weyer. Graduated sizes range from 5¼ inches to 12 inches in diameter.

Overall height of nest is 14 inches. Two of the baskets from the nest are missing. Collection of the Nantucket Historical Association.

The Round Nantucket Basket

The round basket is the starting point for the construction of all styles of Nantuckets. While differences exist in the shaping of the uprights (staves) for the oval form, most fundamentals are the same for all styles. Learning to make a round basket will introduce you to nearly all the construction features of every other basket.

Some readers will choose not to make a few of the elements described in this chapter. The parts most commonly avoided—wooden handles, rims and moulds—can be purchased. I usually include lists of suppliers in the back of my books, but this information becomes dated quickly. Should you wish a tool and supply list, send your request to John McGuire, 398 South Main St., Geneva, NY 14456-2614. Please include a long, self-addressed envelope with two stamps.

While not as refined as the smaller versions of the Nantucket basket, this large utility basket still exhibits quality and durability. Collection of the Nantucket Historical Association.

Above: Nesting set of round Nantucket basket moulds. Collection of the author.

Right: Nesting set of four round Nantucket baskets made by David E. Ray. The antique prices are $1.00 to $4.00. Collection of Olive Hubbard.

Left: Large round Nantucket basket with wooden ears. Collection of the Nantucket Historical Association.

Below: Round Nantucket basket with carved wooden ears. Collection of Charles and Barbara Adams.

Weaving the Round Nantucket

The weaving of all Nantucket baskets is basically the same. The basket should conform to the mould. The weaving is done leaning over the mould and on the far side, NOT in front of you. This process allows you to press the stave against the form and weave it into position with the taut cane. Blisters may appear on your hands, but they will eventually toughen. Use a bandage to protect the area if you feel discomfort. Strength in pulling is not required; in fact such strength frequently distorts the angle of the uprights. Should you find removal of the basket from the mould difficult, place the molded basket in your freezer for a short while. The basket should remove easily. Do not pull it off unevenly, as that will distort the appearance.

Base and Inserting Uprights

Center the disc of wood created for the bottom and secure it to the block using a thumb screw and wing nut protected by a rubber or leather washer. Remember, your decorations are on the inside of the basket. If the groove cut in the base is too low to allow you to insert the staves easily, you can shim the base up with washers.

There are two methods of inserting the dampened (not dripping wet) staves. Some begin to weave and then insert the staves. I find that until you understand the spacing and the numbers required, it is safer to insert all the staves and then check the spacing by pressing the moistened staves against the block. Some makers then allow the staves to dry in place to help conform them to the mould. I find that by making your own stave material and weaving correctly with the moistened staves, you can eliminate this practice.

Soak the cane for no more than five minutes. If you have soaked a quantity of material, keep it in a damp towel rather than letting it dry out and then resoaking it. Repeated soakings ruin the cane. Some people add 1/4 cup of fabric softener to the water. To prepare the cane for weaving the first few rows, thin the back (fleshy) side of the cane with a knife, scraping away some of the material. (The motion is similar to that of curling a ribbon in gift wrapping.) This reduces the cane and allows it to slip easily into the tight areas created by the close positioning of the staves. This hint can be used wherever your spacing is tight.

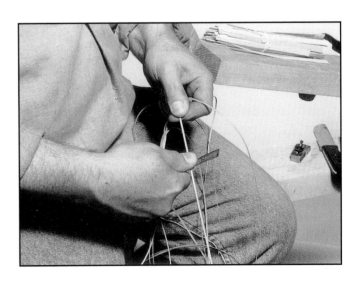

Inserting Uprights

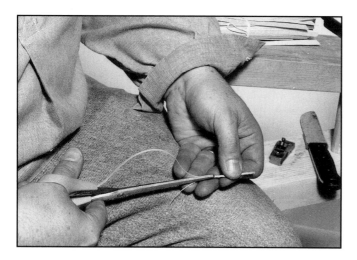

Cut the narrow medium cane (width is up to the maker) to an exaggerated point and insert the tip into the slot.

Cane Widths

▬▬▬▬▬▬▬▬▬▬▬▬▬	carriage
▬▬▬▬▬▬▬▬▬▬▬▬▬	superfine
▬▬▬▬▬▬▬▬▬▬▬▬▬	fine-fine
▬▬▬▬▬▬▬▬▬▬▬▬▬	fine
▬▬▬▬▬▬▬▬▬▬▬▬▬	narrow-medium
▬▬▬▬▬▬▬▬▬	medium
▬▬▬▬▬▬▬▬▬▬▬	common
▬▬▬▬▬▬▬▬▬▬	4mm
▬▬▬▬▬▬▬▬▬▬	5mm
▬▬▬▬▬▬▬▬▬▬	6mm
▬▬▬▬▬▬▬▬▬▬▬	slab rattan

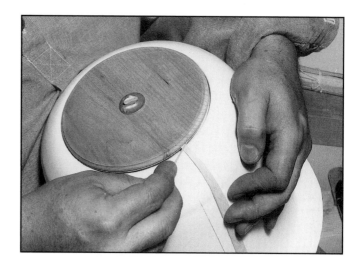

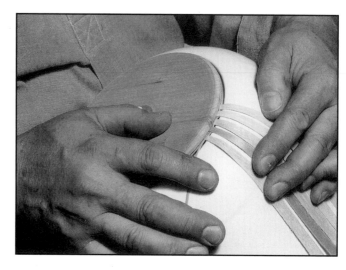

Insert the narrow end of the moistened staves into the slot, and remember: The beveled edge is to the outside of the basket. The staves are inserted so that the pointed ends lie on a direct path to the center. Be careful to check that they are fully inserted, and keep rechecking their tightness as you begin to weave. Don't get the base too wet, as it can warp. Should your taper seem too great, merely cut off part of the tip. If the staves are too thick, sand or thin the back side of the tapered end to allow for full insertion into the slot.

Weaving on Plastic/Wooden Moulds

This photo shows what I consider to be the safer method of starting. Insert all the staves (there will always be an uneven number) into the base. In this basket I will end up using 59 staves. They are fractionally less than 1/2″ wide. I suggest making a template to help position the staves in relation to each other (as shown in photo). A 1/16″ spacer template will work. You do not want the staves to be so close that they overlap at the top of the basket. Careful positioning is essential.

To be sure of a secure fit, I insert all my staves dry and then soak the parts of the staves that need to be pliable to conform to the hard curve of the mould. If the entire stave is soaked, it swells and is harder to

insert fully into the groove. You should experiment to find the method that works best for you. I periodically sponge the staves as I work to prevent their breaking during weaving. Staves prepared with regard for the growth rings are unlikely to break if they are kept moist in the weaving. Some makers use staves made from cane or veneered woods. While this is an alternative, I do not feel it is the best choice.

I use a large rubber band cut from an old inner tube to help check my positioning. It is unnecessary to tie the staves in position to allow them to dry to shape. If you keep the staves damp and press them to the form as you weave, this process is redundant.

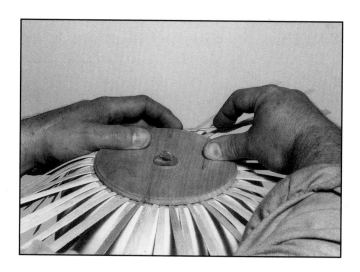

I begin with the elongated, pointed end of the cane and insert the tip into the groove, and then come over the top of the starting stave. Then I weave under the next and so forth until I come around to the start. Because of the uneven number of staves, I next go under the original, or starting, stave.

I weave on the far side of the mould and keep a slight tension on the cane as I weave. After weaving the first few rows, I reposition the staves and check to see that they are still firmly embedded in the groove. I periodically recheck to be sure the staves are vertical and have not worked their way loose.

This photo shows the technique of "hooking" the cane over the tip of my finger to prevent it from twisting as I weave. As you become familiar with the weaving process you establish a tempo, and the work progresses more rapidly.

When you begin to run out of cane or encounter a defect, scrape off the top surface to 1/2 its thickness on the last few inches (a length of 6 staves). The thinned area should begin under a stave, which would conceal this process.

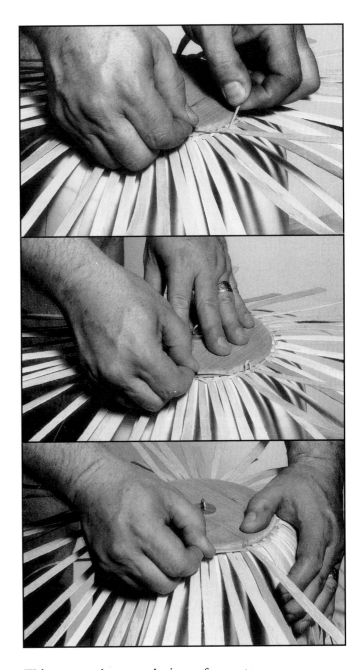

The ending tail stops over the top of a stave.

Thin a new dampened piece of cane to a corresponding length and thickness, using the back side of the cane. Start the joining under the upright and floss it up and under the rib. Pull the end of this covering piece under the stave, hiding the start, and position the remaining cane to lie on top of the lower piece. Overcast the ending tail with the covering cane, and proceed with the weaving until the next piece needs to be added. If this process is done properly, there should be an undetectable join.

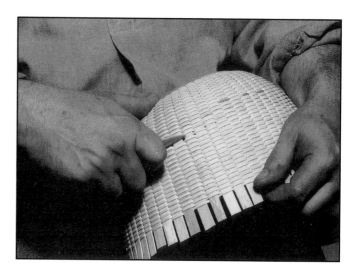

Push the weaving as close as possible to the adjoining rows during the weaving of the tight curve of this basket. Unlike the weaving on the sides, this weaving cannot be compressed. Use a tool to help push the weaving together, and periodically dampen the staves to keep them pliable. Keep rechecking the alignment of the spokes as you weave.

The damp cane will shrink and the basket will compress to the height you wish. Use your fingernails or a tool to help compress the weaving. Do not rush the drying time as your weaving will be loose.

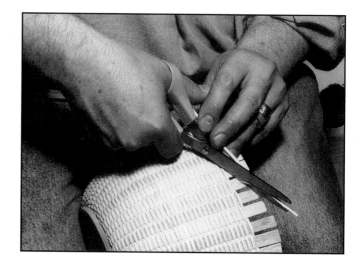

Weave about 1/2″ higher than you wish the basket to be. This basket will be woven to a finished height of 6″. Remove the basket from the mould and let it dry. You can let the basket dry on the mould, but it will take longer.

End the weaving by tapering the end of the cane to an exaggerated point stopping slightly beyond the starting position. The tail end will float inside the basket and will be caught up in the lashing of the rims. There are other alternatives; photographs of several variations appear in the Antique Section.

Placing Rims on the Basket

If your intention is to use metal ears or bone knobs to attach a handle, you may proceed to deal with the rims. If you intend to use wooden ears, they must be carved, notched and positioned before adding the outside rim.

The Inner Rim

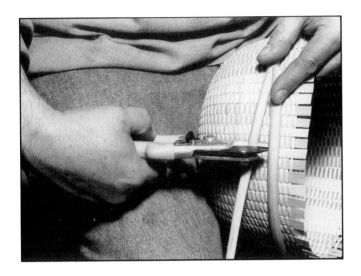

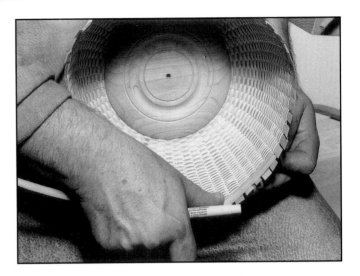

Press the rim material against the inside wall of the basket and allow for an overlap of at least four staves. Mathematically, the outside circumference is the diameter multiplied by pi (3.1417), plus the overlap. Using this formula for both rims will give you a generous inside overlap.

Detail of a Weyer handle. Collection of the Nantucket Historical Association.

In this view I am using commercially available 3/8″ half round reed for rims which overlap at least 4 spokes. If you prefer to purchase a manufactured rim rather than carving one, wooden rims are now available. Some makers cut a birch dowel in half; however, I shall cover the manufacture of wooden rims by hand in the following section.

Soak the reed rim material for about one hour (a small amount of fabric softener in the water will increase its pliability) and let it dry a minimum of a full day after forming.

Placing Rims on the Basket

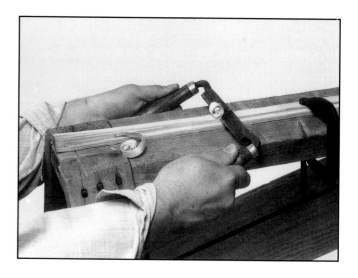

Place the rim in a shavehorse or clamp on a shaving beam created with a modified sawhorse.

Taper the rims, using a drawknife with the beveled edge against the rim. Some people use a belt sander or other tools to create the tapering. Do not carve directly on these marks, as they do not take into account the bulk of the materials.

It is time to fit the inside rim. Stress the rim by forcibly bending it tight, against the basket wall and overlap the piece. Mark the overlapping ends on the opposing surfaces. If you do this correctly one mark will be on the half round and the other on the flat surface.

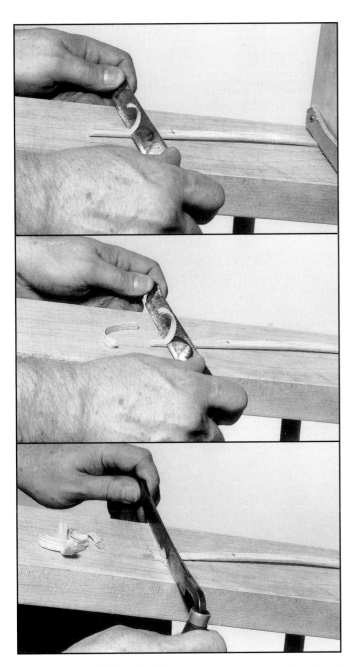

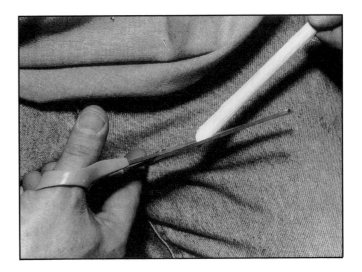

The half round overlapping tip is rounded for appearance.

With the first cut, remove a fractional amount of material. Step outside the first cut and do another shaving. Continue this cautious removal until the final cut profiles the tip into a sliver-thin piece of material. A final scraping holding the drawknife vertically can help smooth any apparent roughness. Now reverse the rim and follow the same procedure on the opposing surface.

Clamp the inner rim in position (the flat surface is against the basket) and be sure the rim rests directly above the last row of weaving. Place the beginning of the overlap on top of a stave for extra support and clamp it in place to prevent slipping. Recheck the look of the basket once the rim is in place. The uprights should not be distorted by the tension of the inner rim. Don't worry if the top is not perfectly round.

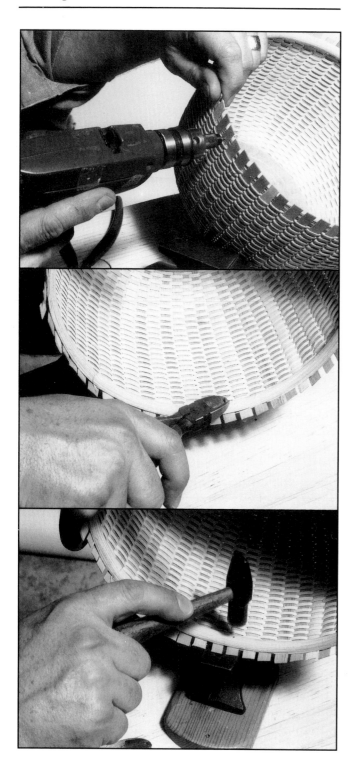

On the outside of the basket and midway from the overlap, drill a small pilot hole with a number 60 drill bit (or smaller). This will allow easy insertion of the 3/4" 20-gauge brass escutcheon pins used in fastening. Hold the rim with about four nails that have been cut flush to the inner rim and then rounded over to secure them. Use a small hammer, wire cutters and an anvil for this process. Tighten the rim against the basket by working toward the overlap equidistantly from the first nail. Should the nails be too loose in the pilot hole, dampen the hole to swell the fibers of the rims to help hold the nail.

Glue the overlap with a cynoacrylate glue or other woodworking glue before cautiously nailing. Be careful not to stick your fingers to the basket with these new high-tech glues. If you use a woodworking glue, be careful not to spread it beyond the work area, as it will affect the appearance of the basket when a finish is applied.

The Outer Rim

Apply the soaked commercial rim, flexed to round, to the outside of the basket. Using a pencil, mark the overlap and taper as previously done on the inner rim.

Stagger the overlaps and again drill and nail the outside rim. Alternate nailing toward the overlap. I make it a rule never to taper the overlaps of the outside rim until I have positioned handles or wooden ears so as to ensure a proper fit. Obviously, brass ears or handles attached on the outside of the rim are the exception, and therefore can be done beforehand. I place overlaps near the handle(s) to take advantage of this extra bit of support, which also helps camouflage the overlaps. Watch the alignment of the rims to be sure they are flush with each other. The number of nails you use is up to you. I usually nail every other or every third upright. When I near the outer overlap, I cautiously glue it together before the final nailing. Remember not to nail the area where you intend to insert the metal ears of your basket.

Metal Ears

Standard Style

When using brass, the ears are shaped from stock available at a hobby store. The thickness should be sturdy enough to stabilize a handle, yet allow you to cut it with sharp scissors or tin snips. The shape for the ear is as photographed. The length of the shank will vary according to the type of handle being installed. Sand or file sharp edges smooth.

On an ordinary handle attachment the rounded brass top protrudes directly above the rim and is inserted into a cut notch created in a handle. Once drilled and riveted, the handle readily pivots on the ears, as shown in this antique example. Occasionally, the handle was not sawn to accept the brass ear but merely attached to the outside.

Low-sided Nantucket basket with swing handle and metal ear, Collection of Charles and Barbara Adams.

Offset Style

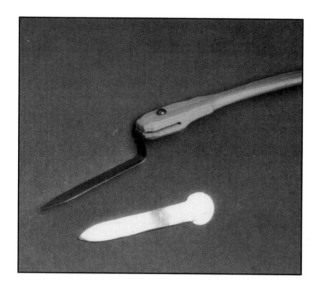

This view shows the heavy annealed brass stock used to create brass ears for a lidded basket.

To allow a lid to be attached to a basket, the brass ears are fashioned extra long and bent to create an offset handle attachment.

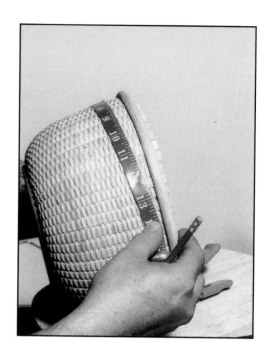

Regardless of which method of fastening the handle you choose, carefully position the ears as close to 180 degrees apart (centered) as possible. Because the basket consists of an uneven number of staves, the handle is slightly out of center. I use a combination of sighting across the center hole of the base with a straight edge, and measuring, to help check the position and then mark the locations with a pencil.

Positioning Ears

Inserting Ears

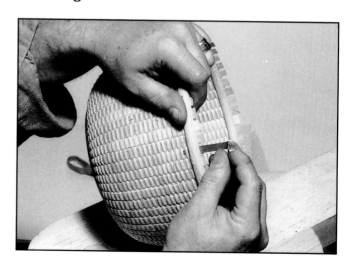

Fastening

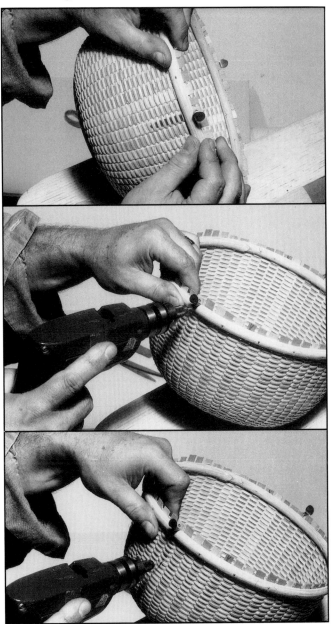

Clip all protruding uprights flush to the top of the rim and sand smooth any roughness.

Return the basket to the mould, push it down snugly to re-form the rim to round, and let it dry.

Insert the offset bent ear flush to the rim. Drill through the rim and ear and fasten with a brass escutcheon pin. Drill the inserted end and secure with another brass nail. Repeat this process on the other ear. When drilling, be careful not to use your finger as a support in the path of the drill. Be careful not to break any weavers with the drill bit.

Standard style ears are fastened in the same manner as the offset style.

Carving Wooden Rims

Rims are frequently allowed to spoil the appearance of a basket. They should not appear dominant. Half-round rims 3/8″ wide will look fine for our 9″ basket. The rims on larger or smaller baskets are proportional. I like my rims no greater than 3/16″ thick for a balanced appearance. I split the wood out as I would for any project. The size I will achieve in rough splitting will be as close to the finished dimensions as I dare. The splitting is the same as for any other project. I will halve the wood using the grain or growth rings. The final piece should approach 3/8″ wide and 1/2″ thick, with the growth rings stacked on top of each other and the convex (bark side) rings curved up (out). To get my two pieces for the outer and inner rims, I will finish halving the wood down the growth rings—giving me two 1/4″ thick rims.

Alternate method of halving the rim stock.

Should your stock dimension out differently in width and thickness, all is perhaps not lost. If the width is at least 1″ wide and 3/16″ thick, you may split the rim stock down the grain (across the rings) and proceed.

The fine carving that is needed to square up the edges and smooth the narrow rims to size is done on the shavehorse. Remember, both rims are bent with the convex rings toward the outside of the bend. It is their placement that determines the rounded surface. Unlike most carving, which is done on the concave ring side, the outside rim is shaped (rounded) on the convex side. If you become confused, let the wood dictate the easier bend. Just remember, the growth rings are stacked up parallel to the wall of the basket.

Cut a radius on the rim edges. Remember to check the growth pattern and position on the basket to determine the correct surface.

When carving rims, use a piece of leather to slide the wood into the carving blade. Carve away from the center toward the ends by reversing your rim stock. A small plane can be helpful. The final scraping is done holding the knife vertically and moving the blade very quickly along the surface. Any catches (chatters) are removed in the opposite direction from how they were created. Sand smooth with wet dry paper (not the black paper).

Bending Wooden Rims

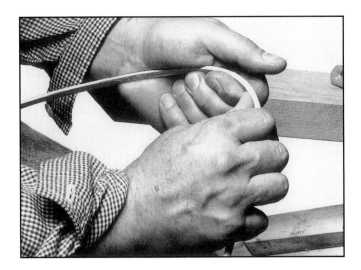

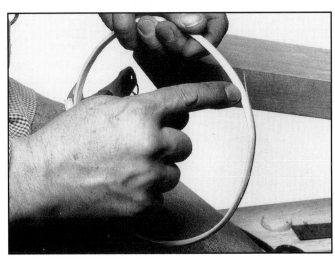

Gently flex the rims, and continue flexing until they easily form a circle smaller than the size you intend them to fit. Remember the flat sides go against the basket. Clamp the rims into a circle and resoak them until you are ready to fit and taper them on the basket. Any resistance to bending evenly is due to an excess of material in that spot. Carve away this excess. Should a sliver of wood lift from the surface, this excess can be scraped off.

Creating Wooden Ears

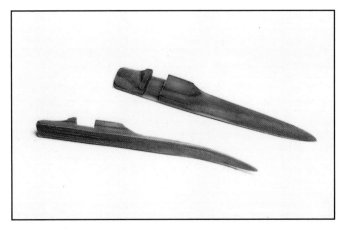

The wooden ears that allow the bail handle to pivot on the basket are the earliest recognizable form of Nantucket handle attachment. Metal ears followed around 1860 and bone or ivory knobs more recently. Some wooden ears were ingeniously created as stave-and-ear combinations. Most were separate pieces inserted into the basket (usually to the outside) after weaving and then held in place with a rim and lashing. This photograph shows the ear notched for our 3/8″ commercial rim and the thin ends, which allow for easier insertion and conformity to the curve of the basket. Like heart handles, ears are created two at a time, split in half for mirrored exactness, and then individually finished.

As with the outer rims, we will carve the ears on the convex surface of the wood. Split the ear stock according to the standard halving rule, and stack the rings of wood on top of one another with the bark (convex) side to the outside. The ear blank should be much longer than the finished piece you need, to allow for easier carving in the shavehorse. Our piece is about 3/16″ to no more than 1/4″ thick. The width is slightly larger than 1″. This width will allow us to split out a pair of 1/2″ mirrored-image ears and give us a waste allowance for safety.

Creating Wooden Ears

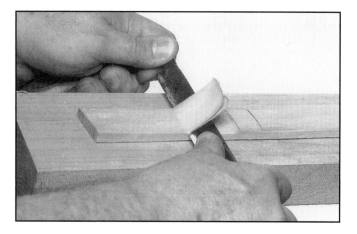

The profile of an ear can vary. Personally, I leave a 1/8" to 3/16" shoulder above and below the anticipated rim and drawknife away the waste. The area where the handle attaches to the ear must be flat to facilitate riveting and thick enough to be sturdy. The top part of the ear that extends beyond the future rim should be no greater than one finished inch in even the largest baskets. Our 9" basket will have an ear that is about 3/4" above the rim, allowing the handle to swing clear of the rim. If the ear sticks up beyond the handle as it rests against the rim, the ear is vulnerable to breaking. Use your drawknife with the bevel against the wood as pictured.

While a matter of taste, the shoulder area which accepts the rim is usually no greater than 1" on the larger baskets, and proportionally decreases on smaller sizes. I fre-

quently position the actual rim against the ear stock and mark a minimal shoulder area for carving references. Once you have created the upper ear, reverse the ear blank and carve the tab of the ear which is inserted into the weaving. I always carve with the bevel of the drawknife against the wood, and make this feature at least 2" long. I severely carve the taper away from the shoulder to a paper-thin end, which allows for an easy fit into the basket. Don't forget to skip an inch of weaving when inserting wooden ears and to cut only these ear staves flush to the weaving. If you have done this process correctly, the profile of your work should approximate this photograph.

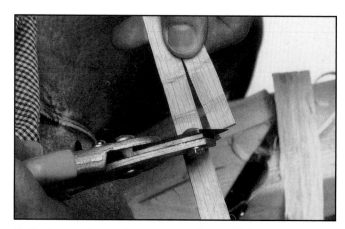

Split the ear down the center and cut off the excess.

Point the end of the tapered tab to allow for easier insertion.

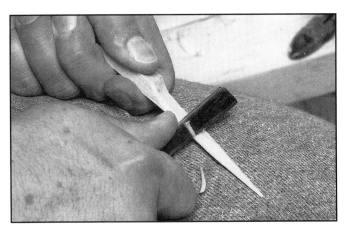

Bevel the edges.

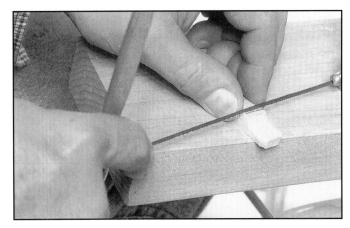

Saw 2/3 through the ear inside the marked lines.

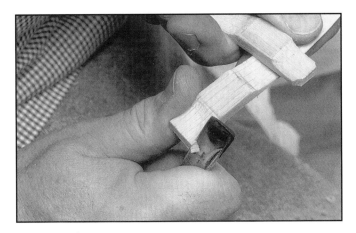

Remove any sharp corners and sandpaper the parts.

Notching the Ears

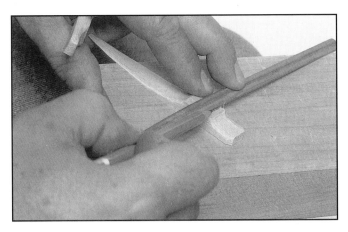

Lay your 3/8″ rim on the shoulder area. Minimize the lug above the rim if the shoulder is too large. Mark the outside edges with a sharp pencil.

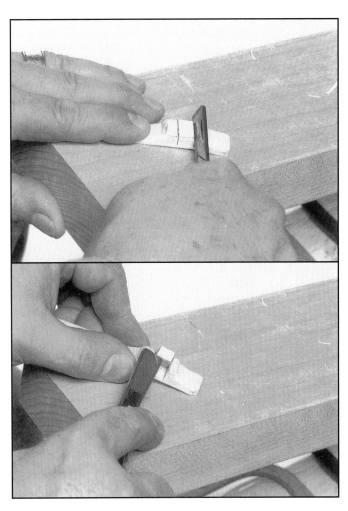

Insert a knife in the kerf of the saw and twist out the waste. Be sure they are cut to the same depth or you can twist the knife and lose the shoulder.

Positioning Wooden Ears

Locate the staves for the ears so they are positioned closest to the middle of the basket. It is important to measure, and not rely only on counting or your eye for aesthetics. Mark the ear staves, check to see that the ears fit, and cut only these staves flush to the cane. Fit your inner rim and overlap the marked and tapered ends close to the ears. Working equidistantly toward the overlap, secure with a few nails. Glue and nail the overlap last. Insert the ears, skipping about 1″ of weaving, and align the bottom of the rim recess so it is flush to the top of the last row of weaving. If the staves are too narrow to accept the tapered end of the ear, narrow the taper to allow for insertion. In large baskets made with very fine staves, this must be done to keep the ears and handle in proportion. Position the outer rim, slightly stagger the projected overlap, and clamp into place. The rim should fit very tightly into the ears. If it is too tight, narrow just the portion of the rim that fits into this recess. Mark the outer rim overlaps on their opposing surfaces and taper the rims slightly away from the pencil lines. Do not taper the outer rim before a final fitting. Reposition and clamp the tapered rim. Now nail alternately toward the overlap. Glue the final tapered overlap and then nail cautiously. Lash as you would any basket; not all Nantucket baskets were double or cross lashed. Remember to press the basket back on the mould to dry.

Note: The number of nails you use in securing the rims is arbitrary. Initially, I use only a few nails alternately added to the basket as I work toward the rim overlaps. Then I add as many nails as I feel the basket warrants. The nails are inserted into a drilled pilot hole using a #62 bit and then are cut flush to the back and gently hammered on an anvil or piece of metal to round the cut end.

Detail of finely carved wooden ear. Collection of Charles and Barbara Adams.

Right: Extremely fine Nantucket round basket. Maker unknown. Note that the ear goes into the base. Collection of the Nantucket Historical Association.

Below: Early six-inch round Nantucket basket with wooden ears. Collection of the author.

Making a Round Lid

Using dividers, find the (centerline) diameter of the basket. This dimension will be the exact center of the rim groove you will turn on both sides of a heavy pine board.

This view shows the shallow straight-sided groove already turned to accept the 3/8″ half-round we have purchased. While wooden rims are more correct, it is extremely difficult to bend wood in this fashion. The pointer shows where the centerline measurement would be positioned. In this project we have used a 1-1/4″ pine board (we need two rims and this thickness allows one on each side of the board) screwed onto a faceplate commonly used in woodturning. The oversized disc has been turned using the same techniques we used in creating the bases. From the predetermined center of the disc, scribe the centerline dimensions on both sides of the board. Using a parting chisel, cut a 3/8″ wide groove that is divided equally on either side of the scribed line(s). The depth and width of this groove must be cut carefully so the reed will fit securely.

Force the soaked rim into the groove and calculate the lengths needed to create the rims with a generous overlap. Use a pencil to mark the locations for the necessary tapering, for which you will use the draw-knife. Remember, the same techniques are used in creating a proper overlap for any rim. Reposition the tapered rims into the groove and cautiously glue the overlaps. This process can be rather tedious but it needs to be done well. Be careful not to get glue into the groove. In order to keep the material in place while drying, I suggest you construct turnbuttons, or buy them at a hardware store.

Note: You can cut grooves of several sizes for different size lids. When you get any proportions correct, write them down for accurate repetition of these processes.

While the rims are drying, begin to construct your lid. The staves I use are extremely wide at the outer ends and dramatically tapered to incorporate the very small knob. The antique baskets seem not to concern themselves with matching the lid and basket staves, in either position or number. However, if you wish to do this, use your basket as a guide and mark your lid mould as a template. Regardless of your approach, careful fitting will enhance the weaving appearance. I also bevel the top edges to make the cane lie closer to the rib.

Weave the lid with cane that is the same width as the cane in the basket. Due to the extremely close positioning of the staves as they wedge into the groove of the knob, I thin the back side of the cane to allow for easier weaving during the first few rows. Some baskets were started with finer cane, and then graduated into the wider weaver. Cut the beginning weaver to a point and start as you would any basket. Remember to scarf your cane on opposing surfaces when joining in a new piece. Watch your weaving tension, as it will affect the look of the lid, which should lie flat. Weave the top larger than required, as the material will pack (tighten) once dried.

Gently pry the rims loose and position the underneath rim to be sure you have a proper fit.

The weaving should stop at the rim junction. Should your weaving continue under the rims, it will produce a wider gap between the nailed rims and could complicate lashing.

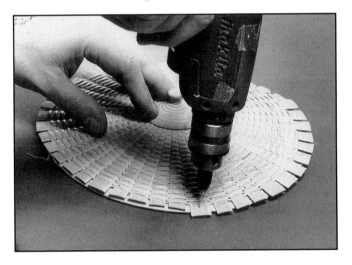

Drill and nail the underneath rim in a few spots to prevent movement when adding the top rim. Sometimes the rims torque a bit in the groove, and you may need to gently force the reed into realignment.

Slightly stagger your overlaps, and then begin to nail the rims together. Drill pilot holes, cut off the excess on the underside, and round the cut ends, using a hammer and a small anvil or piece of metal. On this lid I tend to nail through every stave to help align the rims. Lashing further improves the appearance.

Finely sand the rims to enhance the appearance.

This photograph shows a top view of how the round lid should look prior to lashing and attachment.

Adding Metal Hinges Before Lashing

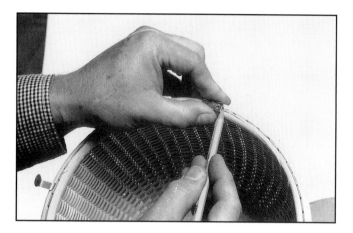

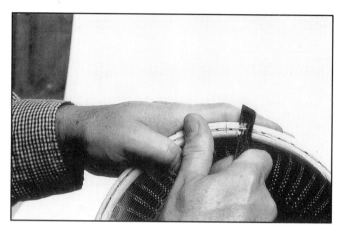

In the center of the rear (back) of the basket, position a 3/4″ fine brass hinge. Mark the position of the hinge by tracing the edges onto the rim of the basket. I squeeze the plates of the hinge closer together with pliers or in a vise to help the lid fit closer to the basket. Some hinges are constructed so that you can remove the pin that holds the hinge together to work with the hinge more easily.

Detail of hinge added to the outside of lidded round Nantucket basket by J. B. Folger. Collection of the Nantucket Historical Association.

Cut a recess (rabbet) inside these lines to a depth that allows the half hinge to lie flush to the rim. Sand away any roughness and fill any gaps in the rim with pieces of wood, to allow better holding of the screws. I further stabilize the hinge by using cyno-acrylate adhesive. I repeat the same process for the lid and, when the lashing is completed, I rejoin the hinge parts with the metal pin we removed earlier. If your hinge is not constructed with a removable pin, the rabbet will show you where not to lash so you can seat the hinge.

Lashing

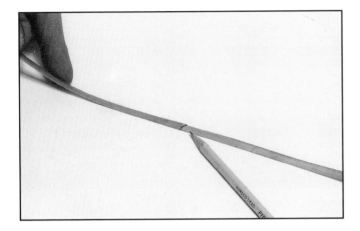

The first step is to determine in which direction the lashing cane can be pulled through the tight spaces without catching the natural ridges which occur in this material. The pencil shows this area. The space between any two rims is covered with wide binder cane sold in metric widths. I use 4mm and cut it to the length needed to overlap itself and scarf the ends. I frequently thin the back side of the wide binder cane to improve its flexibility. It seems to help prevent it from splitting in the lashing process. The length of the lasher can be calculated using the following guide: If your rim is 3/8″, count every space between the staves and multiply it by 1-3/4″. This length will lash your basket. Rims that are 1/2″ need 2″ of cane per space for binding your basket. To cross lash, double these lengths.

The lashing is the size of the cane with which you wove the basket. I frequently cut an additional piece of the weaver, which I use to help finish the edge where the rim meets an upright. These carefully selected pieces are soaked for 5 minutes and then pulled through a sponge or wet towel to keep them from drying during lashing.

Start at or near an ear, fold over the beginning end 1/4″, and force this bulk under the front rim and between a stave. A small wedge can be used to prevent it from being dislodged. Begin to loosely lash through the spaces between the staves. Thread into the loops the top filler and the underneath piece and tighten the lasher.

Open up the tight spaces with an awl and lash the basket from the inside to the outside. When you use wooden ears, you can cut the filler pieces and carefully lash them in place to prevent slipping. You may glue the cut ends if necessary. Some makers fit the cane around the ears. In cross binding you then reverse the direction after lap joining the fillers and create the X-bound look on the top edge of the basket. The X-bound look on the ears or handles will be located on the side.

Lashing

Not all baskets are cross bound. To single lash a basket, overcast the rim through each space between the staves. When you reach the ear or handles, cross over this part and come through the opening as usual.

Reverse the lasher, cross behind the ear on a diagonal, and come through the same hole as shown on the inside. The appearance should be as photographed. Look at the "Antique Baskets" section for hints as to how to vary these final steps.

Should your rims be out of alignment when lashing, pry up on the inside or outside of the rim with a pair of pliers, protecting the rims of the basket with leather.

Should you break the damp lashing, slip the rim "filler" to the side and, from the inside, bring the cane up between the rims and glue or wedge securely. Restart it from the front. The ending of the lashing is most frequently done on the inside of the basket. The end is threaded under the tightened lashing and concealed. Some makers bring the lashing to the outside, thread it under the tightened loops, and then conceal it on the underside of the rim.

Making Wooden Handles

For this project I have selected a piece of fresh hickory, which I have soaked in water to increase its pliability. White ash or other straight-grained hardwoods can be used, but be sure the growth rings are dense and flexible. Wood with very fine growth rings that are immediately beneath the bark is frequently poor material and should be removed as waste. The tip ends of wood that have been "water cured" will be discolored, and should also be removed as waste.

For basket handles made out of kiln dried lumber, be sure the lumber has been quarter sawn. The handles can be sawn out and shaped using power tools and then either boiled or steam bent. Frequently these handles need to be larger in proportion than the finer ones that can be made from green wood.

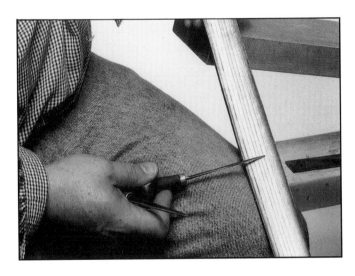

This wood has weathered in the soaking process. Do not confuse this with the bark or heartwood. Remember to split the tree from the top toward the bottom and always halve your pieces. Remove the heartwood after splitting the tree into eighths. Continue halving the wood either down the grain or with the growth rings until the wood is about 1" wide and 1/4" to 3/8" thick. This allows the wood to bend correctly without fracturing it. Should your splitting run off center, put harder pressure on the thicker side and nurse the crack back toward the middle. In finer subdivisions I use a hunting knife and twist the blade from side to side. This acts as a smaller froe. Don't travel the crack too quickly! Splitting is a controlled process. The rings should stack on top of each other with the convex curve to the outside (top). Wet the rings to highlight their growth pattern and don't be confused by saw cuts. Remember, the bark side of the tree is to the outside of any bend.

Handle Length

Handle lengths vary according to the function of the basket. The formula of "1/2 the circumference of the basket plus 1"" allows the handle to rest on the rim, and produces a slightly squared look. A 2" addition to the half-circumference measurement gives a very pronounced "D" handle that rests fully on the rim. Some handles are simply 1/2 the circumference. Purse handles are quite different in proportion. They should allow the arm to comfortably clear the lid and the lid to open easily. Make a template to get the look you are after.

Handle Width

The handle at the point where it joins the ear is about the width of the staves, or perhaps slightly wider if the staves are very fine. It can be shaped to graduate to a wider middle and narrowed on the ends. Shapes vary according to the maker, particularly with the lug areas of the handles where they are riveted. The "Antique Baskets" section should give you inspiration and show you the sophisticated understatement on sizes.

Tips on Carving Handles

Remember, to even out a piece of wood, carve from the middle toward the ends. Due to its growth pattern, one end of the wood is thicker than the other; hence, less wood is removed in one direction than in the other. Use the beveled edge of the drawknife against the wood, and carve away from the heavier areas toward the area you wish to be thinner. You should be carving on the concave side of the growth rings to bend the handle properly. If you are creating a grip, or "boss," in the center of the handle, this section retains full thickness. The ends of the handles are also heavier for riveting. The carving rule here is drawknife away from the heavier areas and take it slowly. Frequently, heavier handles that appear on newer baskets are made by bandsawing dried lumber and then steam bending the material. Green wood carving is not that difficult, makes your work more authentic, and requires less investment in machinery.

Making Wooden Handles

Handle Layout

The center grip area (not required) is no more than 3″ wide for our 9″ basket. Using a soft lead pencil, lay out the grip on either side of the centerline of the handle blank, which has been cut at least 2″ longer than its projected finished length.

I find it helpful to make a pattern (template) with scrap cane, which I can form to the basket to help visualize the handle and its layout.

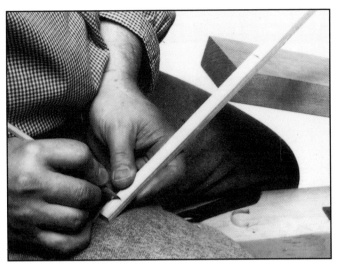

The shoulder that receives the rivet is usually no more than 1″ in length and is clearly defined in carving.

Handle Carving

This view shows the profile the handle should resemble.

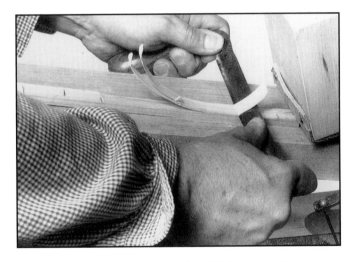

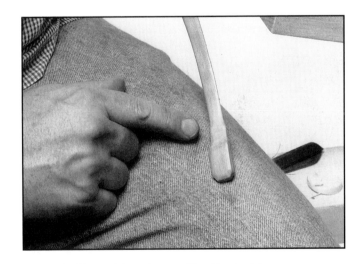

In carving these handle features, I remove a small amount at a time and reverse the blank frequently to keep the cutting even. Remove your work from the shavehorse and check your progress. Don't work the blank thinner than 1/2 its original thickness. You can use the drawknife in a vertical position to help scrape imperfections smooth. Remember, these measurements should be changed proportionately according to the size of the basket.

Use a knife and bevel or radius the inside edges; soften any sharp angles. Cut off the excess on the ends. Remember, hold the knife still and slide the wood into the knife. Carve the lug area to a shape you feel is suited to your basket and round off the corners. Scrape your cuts smooth and sandpaper to a finished look. Your individual approach to carving can become a signature of your work.

Note: A piece of leather on your knee helps in carving and protects your clothing.

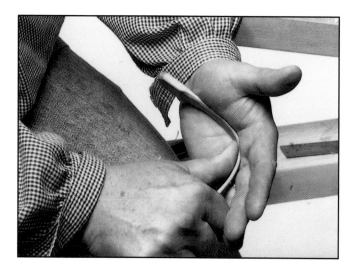

Gently stress the wood against your palm to help square its look, and either attach it to the basket or tie it in position to dry. Some makers use forms to help shape the handle while drying.

This photograph shows how the handle should appear on the basket. When the handle is attached, it should be in balance with the overall aesthetics of the basket. No part should dominate another. If the handle should have a weak spot and changes shape, put a clamped splint on either side while it dries.

Making Heart Handles

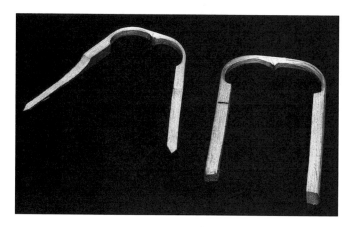

This view shows heart handles in two stages. The left has been tapered to be inserted into the basket and awaits the rim to be fitted into the shoulder or lug area. The one on the right is ready for the taper and rim cuts. Remember, you do not taper the handle on the same side on which you created the heart.

The wood (white oak in this case) is split for this piece the same way it would be for any project. The final dimensions are 1/4″ thick, 1″ wide, and the length that you have determined using a scrap piece of material as a template. Remember to add 2″ extra to help secure the work in the shavehorse. This extra will be removed in the finishing process.

Should you find the width difficult to work with your drawknife, cut the waste away from each edge and then from the center.

The size of antique heart handles was particularly understated. In smaller baskets they spanned only three to four staves and barely allowed room for the fingers to be inserted for carrying. Remember, in positioning the handles on the basket, try to keep them as opposite each other as possible. Wrapped rings can also be used as handles. They are made by coiling a length of splint into a circle and then wrapping it as you would a hinge in a purse. Then secure them in place using cane.

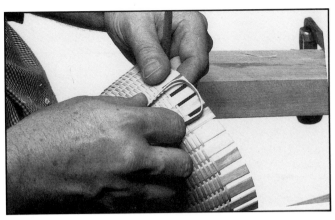

Once you have determined the length of the handle above the rim with your template scrap, mark the rim positions on both ends with a pencil.

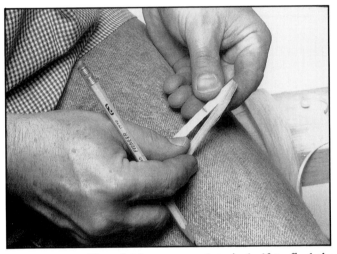

Now fold your template in half to find the middle of the handle area.

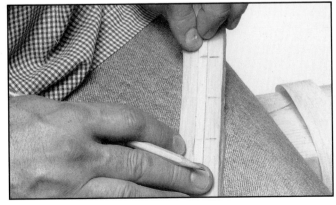

Mark the center and the rim positions on the concave ring surface.

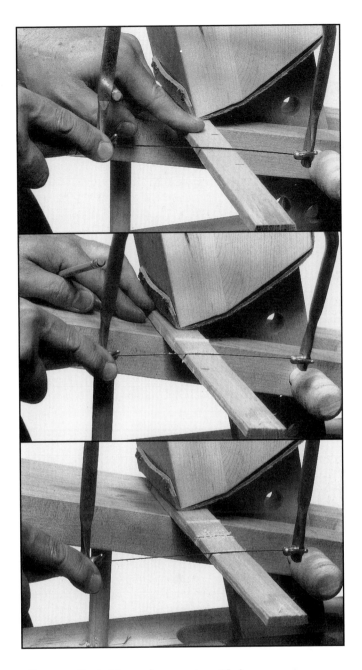

Set an adjustable coping saw to a 45-degree angle. Place your handle blank in the shavehorse jaw and hold it firmly in position. On the centerline saw no more than 1/3 through the wood so that the 45-degree cut slopes toward the end held in the jaw. Then move the saw to the rim line on the far right end. Move inside that line about 1/4" to create a shoulder area and cut 1/3 through the wood, duplicating the direction of the center cut. Reverse the blank in the jaw and repeat these cuts.

Making Heart Handles

If you have done your sawing correctly, the piece should resemble the picture.

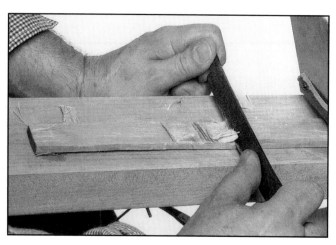

Using the drawknife, carefully remove the waste. Be especially cautious around the peak you wish to preserve in the center. If you are confident that your sawing is exact, you can split away the waste, but it can cost you the peak if you are not accurate. I work with the bevel of the drawknife against the wood and sharply cut away from these saw cuts and toward the center of the two sides of the handle. These severe rounded cuts should reduce the handle to no more than 1/2 its original thickness.

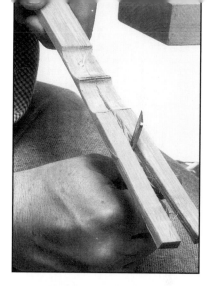

Now split the handle blank lengthwise, using a knife as a mini-froe. If the blank is especially wide you may be able to halve the halves already made. Don't be greedy if you are unsure. Drawknife away the excess rather than risk a disaster.

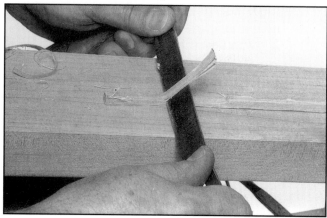

Once you have achieved the look you are after, rotate the handle 90 degrees to create a taper. Leave a maximum 3/4" wood shoulder for fitting the rim. Dramatically taper the ends to paper thin tips and shape them for easier insertion.

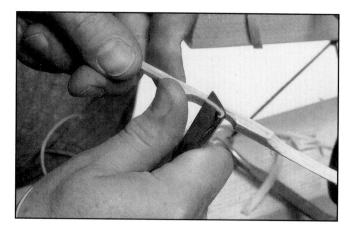

Bevel or radius the inside edges according to your taste and highlight the center peak with your carving.

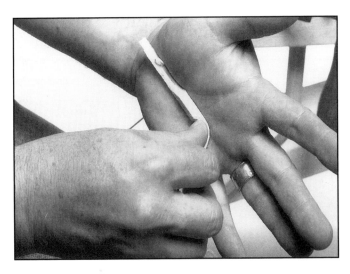

Gently press the corners of the handle against your palm to help shape the handle, and continue to flex the wood toward the lugs (shoulders) so that the handle easily bends into a "D" shape. If the handle fails to bend easily or appears too thick, take some wood off the top edge of the handle. The handle should remain flexible for some length of time before the heat of your hand and drying become concerns.

Check the handle with your basket to see that positioning and shape are correct. Note that handles are not inserted from the top of the basket. Skip about an inch.

Remove the handle(s) and cut flush to the weaving ONLY the staves that the handles are inserted against. This action allows the rims to pull closer together and minimizes distortion. Fit the inner rim as before. Then mark and notch your handles for the outer rim. Use a very sharp pencil and mark the rim widths on the lugs created for them. Inside these pencil lines evenly saw 2/3 through the lugs area. Place your knife in the saw cut and pop out the waste. Be sure the saw cuts are even! If you are unsure of this process, see "Notching the Ears" on page 89.

Fit the outer rim, and nail and glue in position. If you need to review this process, see page 83.

Once the rims are nailed securely, cut the protruding staves flush to the rim and sand any rough places until smooth.

Lash the basket from the inside to the outside. This procedure allows lashing to be pulled tighter than if reversed. See pages 97-98.

Installing a Swing Handle

Wooden Ears

The installation of a handle is dictated by the ears of the basket. If you have a wooden ear the riveting is done according to the following photographs.

Naive Nantucket basket made with unusual discolored cane and wooden ears. Collection of the Nantucket Historical Association.

First locate the center of the flat portion of the ear above the lug. Drill the ear with no larger than a 1/8″ drill. I use a 3/32″ drill and slowly advance the drill through the ear.

Position the bail handle behind the ear and lift it slightly to swing clear of the rim. Mark the position with a lead pencil, using the ear hole as your guide. Drill both ends of the handle. Insert a 3/32″ brass or copper rivet through the hole and slip a burr (washer) over the shaft. Cut the excess flush to the burr. Some people use 2 burrs on each rivet. One is to the outside of the ear; the other is behind the handle.

Gently hammer the cut end round. Be sure just the head of the rivet rests on the anvil when you are pounding.

Metal Ears or Bone Knobs

If you have made metal ears, saw a lengthwise kerf centered in the lugs on the ends of the handle. Make the saw cut deep enough to accept the metal ears. Drill the handle and install it over the secured metal ear to check its ability to pivot freely. Mark the position and drill a hole in the metal to accept the rivet. Sand away any roughness and rivet the pieces together. A burr can be placed on either side of the handle to prevent the rivet from working loose.

Some baskets position the handle on the outside of the metal ear. While this is easier, the basket does not have a polished appearance. If you intend to use bone or ivory knobs, position your 3/32″ or 1/8″ hole so that the handle swings in the center, and carefully drill through the rims. Be careful of hitting the lashing.

Adding a Base Plug

Some makers use a new penny to give a date and to conceal the hole in the bottom. I personally feel this cheapens the work. Because the hole is a standard 3/16″ dowel size, I use a purchased dowel or carve one out of the scrap cherry of the base. Sometimes I use a plastic knitting needle to simulate ivory. Regardless of the material, the method is the same.

Sand smooth and flat the end of the plug you have selected or made. Spin the rod from the outside toward the inside. When the piece touches your finger (placed against the inside hole) adjust it until it is flush. Carefully cut off the excess with a fine saw, cutting in the direction of the grain in the bottom. This is the way you would fill any hole in the bottom. Then sand smooth.

The Oval Nantucket Purse

By now you should have become fairly proficient with the steps necessary for making a round Nantucket basket. Because so many of the steps in making an oval basket are redundant, I will touch only lightly on some that should now be familiar. If you have jumped to this section for your first basket, I suggest you read the steps involved in the previous projects to pick up the details that are abbreviated here. Oval moulds are the most difficult to create. Some people cut a round in half and stretch it to oval. Others use an oval hat mould customized for the job. The biggest problem with both of these alternatives is that the shape is a bit off. I suggest that you treat yourself to a mould. The bases should also be proportional to the size of the basket. I have attempted to give you sizes in the "Antique Baskets" section as a guide.

The oval is considered by many to be the finest shape for Nantucket baskets. Ovals were made in nesting sets, but in far fewer numbers than their round counterparts. The 7″ to 10″ ovals are more commonly found than other sizes. As with any basket made in the lightship era, utility was a big factor. Small forms and miniatures would not have been made in that period. Additionally, the large baskets that today function as picnic hampers and the like were rare. New makers continue to add their creative flair to these baskets and expand their uses. Regardless of the oval's function, its symmetry has universal appeal.

This 18″ oval with double swing handles serves as a carrier. A cloth cover eliminates the need for a lid and allows the beauty of the expansive cherry base to be appreciated. Made by the author.

The oval basket with double wooden lids and a fixed handle is an option in construction. This form provides an opportunity for individual expression. Many makers personalize this form with elaborate inlays of woods. Be creative in your approach to basketry, but remember not to overwhelm the structure itself.

The more contemporary oval purse with its decorated lid is perhaps the most widely recognized form in manufacture today. Many collectors of newer baskets consider the covered oval to be the crown jewel of baskets. The unusual offset handle was a new design created in 1987 by the author.

Above right: Oval nine-inch Nantucket basket with fixed handle and mahogany lids.

Below right: Oval ten-inch Nantucket purse with offset handles.

Oval nine-inch Nantucket purse made with bleached cane.

Purse Decorations: Ivory Alternatives

This photograph shows that found objects, shells and cut stones can be used along with the more traditional bone and ivory. While I am sometimes asked to use ivory, I have a difficult time distancing myself from the poacher that kills for a tusk. Although laws are in place and I deal with reputable carvers, I still have problems with the use of ivory, and have begun to make available synthetic substitutes or fossilized ivory. I feel the sooner we turn away from this material the better. Other materials contributing to the personalizing of the basket seem to be better choices.

Hint: When attaching decorations, be sure that your glue is flexible. This allows natural materials to expand and contract without breaking their bond.

Forming Rims for the Oval

Because I use wooden rims on most of my baskets, I like to pre-form my rims for easier assembly. I clamp these pre-tapered rims to the mould by cutting clamp slots into the flange of my moulds, and I use spring clamps to fasten outside and inside the rims. Because I will weave the basket to the OUTSIDE of this mould, if I fit the rims exactly to the mould they will be too short. Recognizing this fact, I make the rims at least 1/4″ larger than the mould. When they are attached, this "extra" relaxes against the larger basket. This action causes the joins to fit poorly on the mould but properly on the basket. To make them larger, simply drawknife the tapers on opposing surfaces farther from the marks created in calculating the overlap. If you are unsure of this aspect, refer back to the section covering tapering rims. Remember, it is better to have too much than too little! Of course you can always fit the soaked rims to the finished basket, especially if you are using wooden ears which require special fitting. Simply force the basket back on the mould to shape it to oval. Be careful to position it properly on the axis.

Some makers make separate rim moulds by cutting ovals out of wood, and then creating holes to accept spring clamps. The rims are fashioned with generous tapered overlaps, positioned on the side of the oval and then clamped to dry. Should you have only spring clothespins for clamps, wrap the jaw ends with rubber bands to increase their holding power.

Note: Reference marks on rims can be helpful to be sure sizes remain constant.

Making a Stave

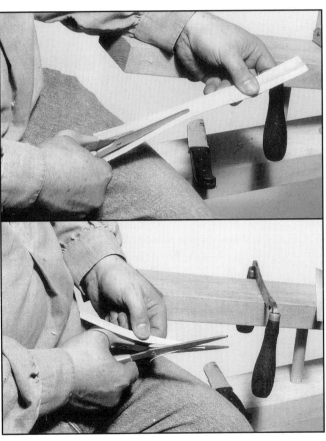

I shape my staves for the oval baskets, covered or otherwise, in the same fashion as for the round baskets (see "Making a Stave," pages 64-66). The full width is now 3/8″ (up to the artist) and the tip is tapered a length of 4″ on both sides in an arcing motion, to gradually reduce the width by at least 1/2. I make my staves extra long so I can customize the fit to the mould and not jeopardize the height of the basket. After fitting, I cut them to an even length for weaving the basket.

The Oval Base

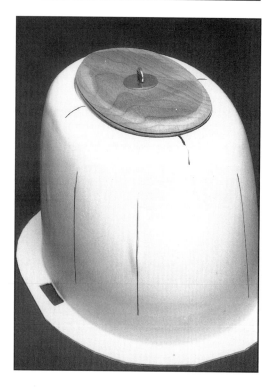

After creating the oval base (see page 60), I attach it to my plastic mould with a 3/16″ thumb screw and wing nut, protecting the base with a washer. I then draw marks on the mould that bisect the oval into quadrants. These fourths are even in size but we need an uneven number of spokes to weave the basket. I "fudge" this by adding the odd spoke where I feel it is least conspicuous. Our horizontal or vertical lines would be the position for center staves on either axis. They function for handle placement or for clasp/hinge locations and should not be changed. In addition, I draw vertical reference lines so I can see if my weaving is pulling the staves out of alignment. Once you achieve the look you wish in this basket you can mark the mould permanently with the number and placement for all the staves.

Note: I created these lightweight plastic moulds to allow makers to ignore problems associated with moisture affecting wooden forms.

Inserting Uprights

You may soak your staves prior to using them, or you can insert them dry and moisten them before you begin to weave. If you pre-moisten the staves you will not want them so wet that they do not fully insert into the groove. Too much water can also cause the base to warp. You can re-sponge the upright when weaving to prevent any possibility of breakage. Remember to recheck the staves as you weave to be sure they have not worked their way out of the groove. Some makers glue them, but then there is no chance for change.

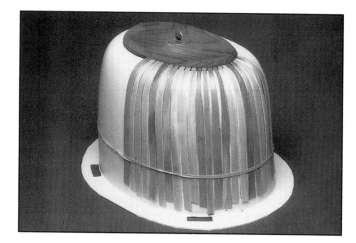

The most demanding step in making an oval is aligning the staves so they appear straight in the mould. Because the arc is greater at the ends of the mould, there will be a need for a larger number of staves to fill this area. You can create a spacing template to make the fit even. Once the arc relaxes you can shorten the tip and change the widths to fit the curves.

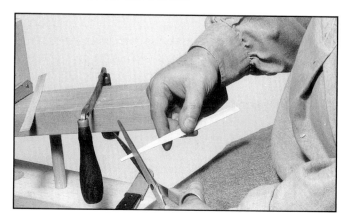

The middle stave on the side is practically straight-sided. Once you have worked one-quarter of the basket the fitting should progress more easily. Check the alignment by holding the now dampened staves against the mould with a rubber band. Remember, don't alter your axis staves and "fudge" in your extra spoke to make the number uneven. If you feel the staves are too close, eliminate some and reposition the uneven number. Take advantage of the natural growth curve of any stave and bevel the top edges to improve weaving appearance.

Note: Remember to make an allowance in the lengths of the staves for customizing. Then cut all top ends even for weaving.

Weaving the Oval Nantucket

Weave the basket as you would a round. Start and finish as you did the beginning projects (see "Weaving on Plastic/Wooden Moulds," pages 75-78). If this is a purse (covered) or a smaller oval I use fine fine or narrower cane for weaving. The height that you weave the basket is up to you. Remember, the weavers shrink a bit and need to be packed.

Placing Rims on the Basket

If your basket is finished (open) and has metal ears or if the handle is attached through the rim as with a purse, you can now fit your pre-formed rims (see "Placing Rims on the Basket," pages 79-83). Drill and anchor the inner rim with a few nails and then glue your overlap, once a proper fit is achieved. The reference marks I suggested can be very helpful.

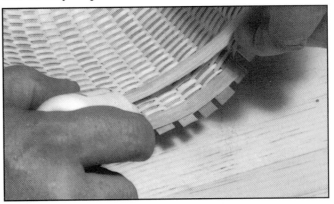

Place the metal ears in position and add your outer rim. Nail equidistantly toward the overlap, tightening as you proceed. (I place both overlaps on the same side.) Glue the overlap and carefully nail it. Add as many #20 escutcheon pins as you wish. Remember to nail the metal ear and nail the tail of the ear pushed into the weaving. If your rims are preshaped there is no need to shape them on the block. Proceed directly to lashing.

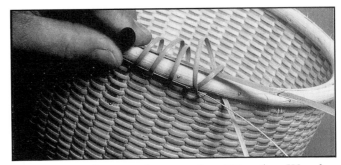

If you are using wooden ears (see "Creating Wooden Ears," pages 87-89), install them on clipped staves and apply the outer rim. Once they are nailed, you may proceed to lash the basket. If the oval is open and has wooden ears, soaked rims may be fitted and the basket dried on the mould.

Making an Oval Lid

As you did with the round lid (page 94), transfer the rib positioning to the top mould. Remember, the size of the oval at the rim is the same, but the shape of the top is quite different. The stave length is obviously not the same as the bottom but the staves can be shaped the same as the basket. You can customize the staves by trimming off the tips (see page 114) to fit the mould and aligning them at the wooden top. I then trim the staves to a length that protrudes beyond the proposed rim. This extra length helps in weaving the lid tight to the mould and allows me to rubber band the ribs against the mould to allow for proper drying. A dry, properly shaped lid allows the rims to be easily added. You should weave with the same width cane as you did the basket.

I mark the lid mould as I did the basket mould so I will not shift alignment. Weave the lid tightly to the form by pressing the dampened stave against the form and weaving in the taut cane. Should you fail to keep it against the form, the lid will not fit the bottom. Remember, weave a little beyond the finished point, as the weaving shrinks slightly and needs to be packed. After drying, I attach the inner rim first with a

few nails and then glue the overlap. Check to see that the lid matches the bottom. Then I nail on the outer rim, tightening equidistantly toward the overlap, glue the overlap, and then carefully nail this last. I put the overlaps on the same side of the basket. If the tapers are done correctly they should be nearly invisible.

If you have pre-formed the parts and let them dry, assembly is much easier and more accurate. The ribs should align with the top in place. By showing such care, you will enhance the look of the finished basket and its lashing.

Hint: Some makers drill the holes for the hinges at this point (pages 119-120) and lash the top and bottom. When they finish the hinges they slide over the cane and install the hinges.

Creating the Wrapped Leather Hinges

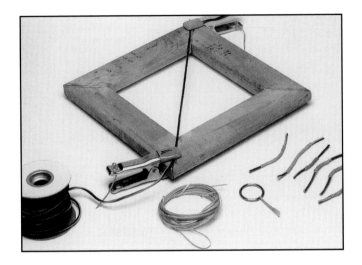

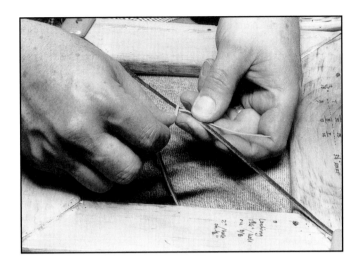

Use the same fine fine cane used for weaving and leather lacing stretched tight inside a wooden frame. This leather is readily available in shops or through mail order. Sometimes I use heavy sheepskin, which is reported to be longer-lasting due to the lanolin.

Note the keyring with the lightweight tin folded around the ring. This is the throat which you push the cane into to pull it under the wraps.

Hint: Give yourself ample leather on either end of the wrapping for pulling it through the rims and fastening. You can wrap the hinges in a series before cutting them free. The way people complete their whipping of hinges is highly diversified. This is only one way of doing them.

Start in the center of the stretched leather and begin your reverse wrapping about 2″ from the beginning of the cane. This becomes a tail you will overcast. Place the short tail, which is headed away from you, on the leather. Reverse the direction of the cane, and then tightly overcast this 2″ tail and leather. Be careful not to get a twist in the hinge.

Cut the soaked cane long enough to complete one hinge and start with the rough side of the leather up. The most number of wraps for a single part is 44, and that is the "centered" front hasp. The numbers of wraps per part are as follows and are based on 3/8″ rims and 1/2″ rims:

3/8″		
	Top	Bottom
Rear	29 (make 2)	13 (make 2)
Front	32	14
1/2″		
	Top	Bottom
Rear	36 (make 2)	16 (make 2)
Front	44	18

117

Creating the Wrapped Leather Hinges

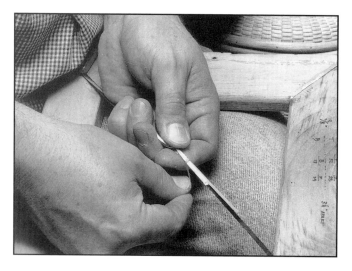

Keep the wraps as close to each other as possible and whip over this tail to conceal it. Count the number of full wraps. When you reach four less than the completed number, stop wrapping, but keep it tight.

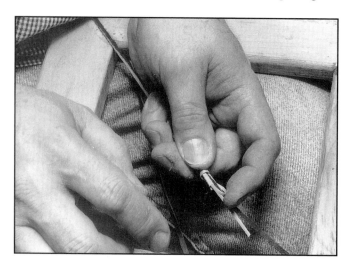

Take a piece of roof flashing tin or the tin of a soda can and cut a strip the width of the leather and about 3″ long. Fold it in the middle and slip it over a ring. Lay this tin in the path of your wrapping and complete the last four tight wraps over the tin, cane, and leather. Wrap the leather one extra loop and cut off the gross excess, leaving enough to pull underneath the wraps. Firmly force the cane end into the throat of the tin.

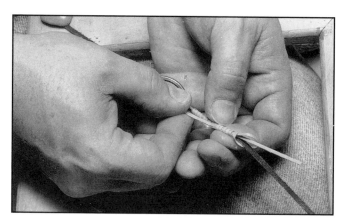

Squeeze the tin to hold the cane and gently pull on the ring. If you do this correctly, the tin will capture the end and pull it underneath the wraps and to the outside. Tighten the wraps by pulling and adjusting gently, and the last extra wrap should pull inside, leaving the finished number desired.

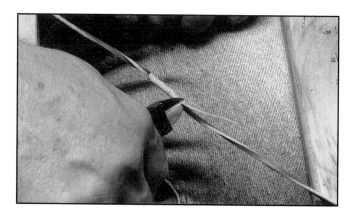

Cut off the excess cane. Skip a generous space on the leather and wrap all the hinges in a series.

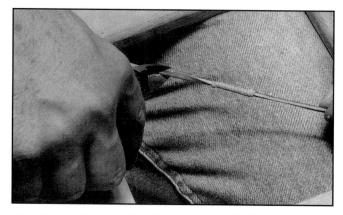

Cut the leather, leaving long ends to help easily form the hinges.

Hinge Placement

In smaller baskets the back hinges are 2-1/4" apart; on larger baskets they are 3-1/4" apart. I place the hinges where the overlaps are found and consider this the back side of the covered oval. If you pre-form the double hinges and glue the ends together, they are easier to manipulate. Also in boring holes between the rims to accept the hinges, a dental or other craft drill is easiest and more accurate to use.

Detail of double-handled treatment on the Nantucket oval bag. Note the ivory latch, pin and buttons. Collection of the Nantucket Historical Association.

First I locate the center of the basket on its side or minor axis. I locate the front center stave for placement of the front hasp and staple for the pin. Some of these assemblies are available in bone or other materials. Their use usually requires the hasp to be woven into place.

Hinge Placement

On either side of the centerline, in the rear, I equally divide the 3-1/4" distance between hinges. I clearly mark these spots with a pencil line that can later be sanded away. A ruler with a straight edge will help in determining the location.

I then reposition the top and transfer those lines to the lid for proper positioning.

The next step is to drill, underneath the rear rim and in between the rims, a hole large enough to accept the leather hinges. If you reverse this process you are drilling blind and can drill through the weaving, creating a real mess. Create a recess in the lower edge of the rim to accept the hinge bulk and allow for a neat lashing. Note that these loops are oriented vertically. All wrapped leather parts are glued and nailed with 20 gauge escutcheon pins to prevent their removal when stress is placed on them. Cut the leather off flush to the top of the rim. Position the loop in the front on a similar vertical axis. This loop (staple) will accept the pin in our latch. Glue and nail the loop and don't forget the recess in the lower edge of the rim. Sand the rim smooth and lash the basket rim using the fine fine cane as a lasher. Remember to fill the void between the rims with wide binder cane. The third piece of "filler" that conceals the join between the rim and weaving adds a special touch but complicates lashing prior to adding the hinges. Refer back to the lashing section for a review of techniques and the formula for figuring the length of the lasher. I join the overlaps in the back of the basket. Remember, covered ovals are seldom cross lashed due to bulk.

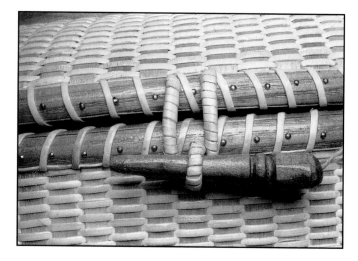

Proceed to the top and drill the holes from the top edges and create the same recesses. The configuration of the assembled hinges varies, and you may duplicate this look or find a design you like in the "Antique Baskets" section. Lash the top.

While other methods are perhaps easier, I wait and do the top last. I find it easier and neater to manipulate the lighter weight lid and lash at this point. You may choose to explore other options.

Hint: As previously stated, many makers predrill the rims for the hinges and then lash. When adding the hinges they slide aside the cane and install the hinges.

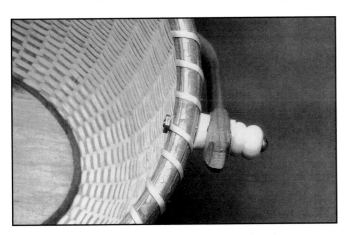

The last step is to fasten the handle (see "Creating a Purse Handle," pages 122-123) with bone knobs (buttons) and washers. The threaded screw is 3/32″ and I suggest a 1/8″ drill, carefully centered on the horizontal (major) axis. Be careful not to drill through the lashing. Assemble the parts as shown and cut the excess thread flush to the rim. File or grind the rough end and do the same with the screw slot to eliminate the groove.

Plug the holes.

Sign the work and date it.

Options

Like all baskets, these are open to multiple variations. Here is a proposed form in process that uses a fixed handle and lids secured to a brace pinned between the handle.

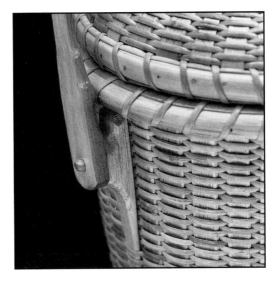

This photograph shows an adaptation for handle treatment that I copyrighted in 1987. Your artistry and creativity are valuable tools for creating your special look.

Creating a Purse Handle

Handles are perhaps the best avenue for individual expression in a Nantucket. Double handles on a handbag or other basket can greatly improve stability and alter the look of your work. Remember that pairs of handles are created by carving a wide piece of wood which can be split lengthwise (down the grain), thus creating a matched pair.

It is important in handles that you familiarize yourself with the growth ring pattern of the wood before carving. The rings of the wood should curve out (convex) and be at the top of the handle. The actual blank of wood should be approximately 3/8″ thick and the growth rings stacked on top of one another.

The profile of the handle is optional; however, many makers like a grip in the center of the handle for interest and comfort. Similarly, the length of a handle is another option. Remember, if they are not long enough the owner cannot carry it easily. I find that a finished length of 22″ appears fine for a 9″ covered oval. This handle is installed on the major axis. Double handles are installed on the minor axis and the same considerations would be followed. The "Antique Baskets" section will help you with their look and placement.

Split out a piece of handle stock at least 24″ long. The extra length, which is cut off later, helps in securing the ends into the jaws of a shavehorse or allows clamping on a shaving beam. Much of the carving techniques are the same as those found on pages 99-100. Take special care to carve on the concave surface of the wood. The lugs at the ends of the handle can be longer than those on a regular handle; however, the grip remains gently tapered away from a 3″ center. I suggest you make a template and keep it for further reference.

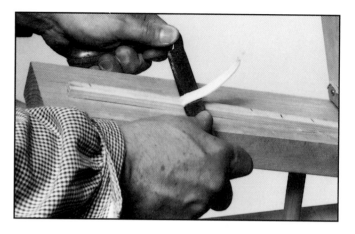

The roughed out handle is hand carved with a jackknife and leather is used for sliding the wood into the stationary cutting blade. Whittling creates a choppy look and can produce gross irregularities. Soften the top edge and radius the inside edge for comfort in the hand. Sand smooth any irregularities and burnish with a soft scouring pad or wood shavings.

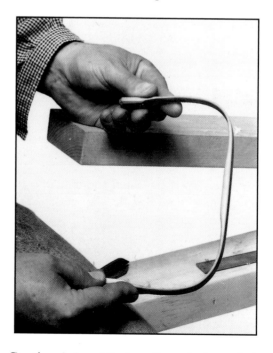

Cautiously bend the handle at the intended corners. Keep your bending controlled if you wish to create a "D" look. If you flex the wood too close to the grip it will resemble a hoop. At this point I frequently apply the handle directly to the basket and let it dry. A separate form can be created to shape the handle before attachment. Remember to tighten the handle fasteners a second time if it is applied wet. The wood will shrink.

Handle mould with assorted bases.

Finishes

It appears that the earliest baskets were shellacked to improve durability, probably as a logical extension of a maintenance requirement of a ship's "brightwork." Varnish was the later of the two finishes. Now urethane, which I dislike, seems to be the favored finish. I carefully polish the "look" of my baskets to be sure they are ready for the final step. I fine sand all rough spots and clean the basket with a brush dipped in wood alcohol. I burnish any wood features with a soft scouring pad or wood shavings.

You can purchase shellac in dated cans. These dates are accurate, and the shellac should not be used after the expiration date. You can also make your own, using shellac flakes and denatured alcohol. Don't use thick coats.

First I mix 20% orange shellac with clear and add enough alcohol to thin the mixture for a finer finish. Use a good brush, not a foam brush, and carefully finish all parts. I start on the inside and work out. This step is optional and done to add an immediate warmth to the basket. Let the basket dry.

All subsequent coats of finish are done with thinned clear shellac. The whole basket is re-coated except for the inner weaving and staves. This omission allows the basket to breathe.

Fine sand between coats but be careful not to go so deep as to remove the first coat with the orange pigment.

Do as many coats of finish as you wish, but remember to let them dry thoroughly before doing another.

Enjoy!

Covered oval Nantucket with unusual low "carrying handle."

Glossary

Aft: Rear.

Alignment: Position or place in line.

Algonquian: Language spoken by Algonquian tribes.

Anglican: Pertaining to or characteristic of the Church of England.

Aniline: The base of many coal-tar dyes.

Annealed (brass): Brass that is heated and slowly cooled to prevent brittleness and increase toughness.

Anvil: A heavy metal block of iron or steel which can be used to round over cut ends of rivets or nails.

Arced: Refers to a rounded undercut shape used for a foot on a base.

Axis: A straight line through the center of a solid figure or body, around which the figure rotates.

Bail: Semi-circular handle of a basket, pail, kettle, etc.

Ballast: Heavy substance such as stone laid in the hold of a vessel to steady it.

Bandsaw: A saw consisting of an endless toothed belt mounted on wheels.

Bark: A sailing vessel of three or four masts, square-rigged except for fore and aft.

Beached: To be cast ashore, not employed at sea.

Beveled: Inclination of two surfaces other than at right angles; to slant, to chamfer.

Binder cane: A wider cut cane, sold in millimeters. In our craft it is used for concealing the space between rims.

Black ash *(Fraxinus nigra):* A hardwood tree used in the making of baskets.

Block makers: Tradesmen who created pulleys.

Bone knobs (buttons): Lathe-turned decorative shaped pieces used in handle assembly; available in bone, ivory, synthetic and fossilized materials.

Brad point drill: Special drill bit with a pointed center for easy positioning.

Brig: A two-masted ship square-rigged on both masts.

Brightwork: Parts or articles to which polish or finish was applied.

Bulwarks: The raised side of a ship, above the upper deck.

Burnish: To polish by friction, to make shiny.

Buoy: A warning marker (float) fastened (moored) on a dangerous rock or shoal.

Cane: The inner bark of rattan that is cut into narrow strips and used for weaving. The finest width is carriage fine with sizes graduating up to super fine, fine fine, fine, narrow medium, medium and common. Larger is sold in millimeters.

Chisel: See **Parting** or **Slotting**.

Circumference: The boundary of a circle.

Concave: Hollow and curving inward.

Conjunct: Act of joining together (intersect).

Convex: Curving outward; in wood, the side closest to the bark.

Cooper: A person whose trade is the making and repair of casks, barrels and buckets.

Coping saw: A narrow-bladed saw set in a recessed frame and used for cutting curved pieces from wood.

Corinthian: Greek architecture characterized by ornate, bell-shaped capitals (the upper members of pillars).

Cynoacrylate glue: Similar to "super glue."

Diameter: A straight line passing through the center of a circle.

Dividers: A pair of compasses or compass-like devices used for measuring.

Divvying: To divide up, to give a share.

Drawknife: A double-handed tool with a cutting blade used in fashioning wooden parts; used by drawing toward the user.

Drift whales: Dead whales that floated onto a beach.

Ears: The projections of either metal or wood on which the handle pivots. Small side handles are also referred to as "ears" in basketry.

Drill: See **Brad point drill**.

Escutcheon pins: Fine brass nails fashioned to fasten ornamental plates about a keyhole; used to fasten rims and secure brass ears in Nantucket basketry.

Estuary: A wide mouth of a river where its currents meet the sea and are influenced by tides.

Fathom: Length of 6 feet, or 1.829 meters.

Fine fine cane: A width of cane that is used for finer appearance, frequently used in Nantucket purses (see **Cane**).

Foot: The lower part of a wooden base.

Fore: At or near the front.

Forms: Blocks or moulds used to weave baskets to size and shape.

Friends: Quakers.

Fumigation: To subject to smoke or fumes for destroying vermin and insects.

Galley: A long, low vessel used in ancient and medieval times, propelled by oars and sails, or oars alone.

Gam: An exchange of visits between whaling vessels and crews; a social visit.

Glycerine: A sweet, oily, colorless alcohol.

Gouge: Lathe tool with a rounded end.

Greasy luck: Slang for money.

Greek Revival: A style of architecture in the early 18th and 19th centuries using modified Greek elements.

Grounds: An area or tract of the ocean.

Hacksaw: Fine-tooth saw used in cutting metal.

Hasp: A hinge that passes over a staple and is secured by some device.

Heart handle: A side handle (ear handle) that has a central interior pointed shape which is reminiscent of the top portion of a stylized heart.

Heartwood: The darker center section of a tree which is the tree's metabolic storage area.

Hold: The area below deck where cargo is stored.

Ionic: An order of Greek architecture characterized by a capital with scroll-like ornaments.

Irons: A nickname given to harpoons.

Ivory: The tusk of an elephant or walrus, or the tooth of a sperm whale.

Joining: To join or overlap two ends during weaving; an area of attachment.

Keep sweet: To keep sound or free from decay; to preserve.

Kerf: A cut or notch made by a saw, axe, etc.

Kerosene: Fuel oil derived from crude petroleum.

Kiln-dried lumber: Lumber dried in carefully controlled drying ovens (lumber is also air-dried).

Lashing: The process of binding rims together with lasher; can be single or double (cross bound).

Lathe: A machine that holds and spins metal, wood or plastic so that when the operator holds abrading tools against the materials, they are cut and shaped.

Lay: A share of the cargo.

Lightship: A ship used as a floating lighthouse.

Loyalists: Those loyal to the King of England.

Lug: Projection or shoulder (thicker area); used in reference to handle profiles.

Maritime: Of or pertaining to the sea, its commerce or navigation.

Mooring: To secure a ship in one place, as with an anchor or with cables attached to shore.

Nantucket sleighride: The highly dangerous "ride" produced when a harpooned whale attempts escape.

Nesting: Referring to baskets made to fit inside one another for economy of space.

Parting chisel: A lathe tool used to cut off a portion of the main piece.

Patina: A surface of antique appearance.

Pi: Mathematical term referring to 3.1417.

Polyethylene glycol (PEG): A waxy substance that can be dissolved in water and used to rejuvenate excessively dry wood.

Polymer: Any two or more compounds formed by polymerization; the combination of the two substances changes the molecular arrangement.

Polyurethane: A synthetic finish.

Portico: A porch, open space or ambulatory with roof upheld by columns.

Potassium permanganate: A chemical used as an oxidizing (darkening) agent.

Powder post beetles: Wood boring insects evidenced by tiny holes and powdery wood residue; fumigation is required.

Puritans: English Protestants who advocated a simpler creed and ritual in the Church of England in the 16th and 17th centuries.

Quaker/Quakeress (male/female): A member of the Society of Friends; originally a term of derision, it derives from the founder's admonition to tremble at the word of God.

Quarter sawn: Boards cut from logs that have been quartered so that each face corresponds to the log's radii.

Rabbet: A recess or groove cut into the edge of a piece of wood.

Radii: Plural of radius.

Radius: A straight line from the center to the circumference of a circle or sphere.

Rattan: A climbing palm used in the production of furniture or cut and processed for reed and cane.

Reference mark: A mark used to line up parts or to reposition them in the same fashion.

Rib: Stave or spoke.

Riggers: Tradesmen who installed the cordage of a ship, including that used as cranes, scaffolds and slings.

Rim: Half round or flat oval pieces of wood, reed or other material, used for the top of a basket, against which the handle rests and attaches; refers to both inner and outer positions.

Riving: A term used in reference to splitting out wood; for example, ribs of a basket are rived by successive halving of wood down the growth lines (rings).

Roof flashing: Thin metal used in roofing.

Sapwood: The newer, fresher growth of a tree, lighter in color and closer to the cambium layer of the tree which produces annual growth.

Scarf: A lapped joining created by tapering opposing surfaces of the material to be connected.

Schooner: A fore-and-aft rigged vessel with two or more masts.

Screw center: A lathe accessory that has a tapered end to fit into the lathe and a platform and screw to tighten materials against for turning.

Scrimshaw: Bone or ivory products decorated with incised (engraved) designs highlighted with dark agents such as India ink; some scrimshaw is polychromed (colored).

Scrimshawing: Doing mechanical work.

Scurvy: Swollen and bleeding gums caused by a lack of vitamin C in the diet.

Selectman: One of a board of town officers with executive authority in local affairs.

Shavehorse: A foot-operated clamping device used to hold wood in position while using a drawknife.

Shaving beam: A flat wooden surface on which wood can be clamped for carving.

Shellac: A varnish-like solution of shellac flakes dissolved in denatured alcohol and used as a transparent coat on a surface.

Shoal: A shallow place in a body of water.

Shooks: Small areas in the hold; specialized barrels were made to fit these compartments.

Skew: A cutting tool used with the lathe.

Sloop: A single-masted fore-and-aft rigged sailing vessel.

Slotting chisel: A hollow ground tool created to prevent binding when a slot is being cut in a base for the staves of a basket.

Spermacetti: High-quality oil from the sperm whale, used for candles and lamp oil.

Splint: Wood prepared by dividing along growth rings with a froe, axe, wedges, hatchet or other splitting device.

Spokes: Vertical elements of a basket; for our purposes, the uprights of a basket.

Spreaders: Bars of wood extending from the yardarm on which early lightship lanterns were hung.

Staple: A "V"-shaped piece used to secure a hasp.

Staves: The curved vertical side elements of a Nantucket basket; sometimes referred to as ribs, spokes or uprights.

Stud: A small protuberant ornament created in the making of a knob.

Tallow: A mixture of hard animal fat refined for use in candles or soap.

Taper: To narrow or gradually thin toward one end.

Taut: Tight, pulled snugly.

Template: Pattern.

Thumb screw: A screw that can be tightened with thumb and fingers.

Toolrest: A metal rest against which lathe tools are held in cutting.

Torque: Anything that causes the action of twisting or rotation.

Try works: A furnace where the carcass of a whale is rendered.

Turn buttons: They pivot on a screw and hold in position a drying circular rim; frequently used to hold screens or storm windows in position; available in metal, they can also be fashioned in wood.

Varnish: A solution of gums or resins in alcohol, used as a transparent coat of a surface.

Vertical: At right angles to a particular point of surface.

Wampanoag: Eastern Massachusetts tribe speaking Algonquian dialect.

Weavers: The woven horizontal elements of a basket; the material for Nantuckets is usually cane.

Wing nut: A nut with wing-like projections used to tighten nut with thumb and fingers.

Yard: Long slender tapered spar set crosswise on a mast and used to support sails.

Yardarm: Either end of a yard of a square sail.

Photographs by Dale Duchesne: pages 66, right; 100, left; and 110.

Illustrations pages 34 and 35 by Margaret Davidson.

Bibliography

Bliss, William Root. *Quaint Nantucket*. Boston: Houghton Mifflin Co., 1896.

Carpenter, Charles H., and Mary Grace Carpenter. *The Decorative Arts and Crafts of Nantucket*. New York: Dodd, Mead and Co., 1978.

Chase, Helen Winslow. "Nantucket: 'The Grey Lady.' " Nantucket Guide. Nantucket, Massachusetts: 1989.

Coffin, Patricia. *Nantucket*. New York: Viking Press, 1971.

Cook, George Crouse. "The Evolution of the Lightship." Paper presented to the Society of Naval Architects and Marine Engineers, December 1913.

Crosby, Everett U. *Books and Baskets, Signs and Silver of Old-Time Nantucket*. Self-published, 1940.

Flayderman, E. Norman. *Scrimshaw and Scrimshanders, Whales and Whalemen*. New Milford, Connecticut: Self-published, 1972.

"The Friendship Baskets and their Maker, José Reyes." Brochure. Nantucket, Massachusetts: 1960.

Gambee, Robert. *Nantucket Island*. New York and London: W. W. Norton and Co., 1986.

Gardner, Grace Brown. Scrapbook. Nantucket Historical Association Collection, Volume Nine.

Guba, Emil F. *Nantucket Odyssey*. Self-published, 1965.

Kobbe, Gustav. "Life on the South Shoal Lightship." *The Century Magazine,* August 1891.

Kugler, Richard. *The Whale Oil Trade 1750-1775*. New Bedford, Massachusetts: Old Dartmouth Historical Society, 1980.

Macy, Obed. *The History of Nantucket*. Boston: Hilliard Gray and Co., 1835. Reprint. Ellinwood, Kansas: Many's, 1985.

Macy, William F. *The Story of Old Nantucket*. Boston: Houghton Mifflin Co., 1928.

Pacific National Bank of Nantucket 1804-1979: A Remarkable Bank Account. New York: Fred Gardner Co., 1980.

Seeler, Katherine, and Edgar Seeler. *Nantucket Lightship Baskets*. Nantucket, Massachusetts: Deermouse Press, 1972.

Starbuck, Alexander. *The History of the American Whale Fishery*. Argosy Antiquarian Limited Reprint, 1964.

————. *The History of Nantucket*. Boston: C. E. Godspeed and Co., 1924.

Starbuck, Mary Elizabeth. *My House and I*. Boston and New York: Houghton Mifflin Co., 1929.

Thompson, Frederic L. *The Lightships of Cape Cod*. Maine: Congress Square Press, 1983.

Whipple, A. B. C. *The Whalers*. Alexandria, Virginia: Time Life Books, 1979.

Additional reference sources include United States census records, United States Coast Guard, Lightship files, proceedings of the Nantucket Historical Association, and personal interviews with Lauretta Gibbs of Nantucket Island, Douglas Porchette of Clifton Springs, New York, and Henry G. Kehlenbeck, president of the Pacific National Bank in Nantucket, Massachusetts.

Stereoscopic view labeled "Old Hermit" from Nantucket Island. Author's collection.

INDEX